CENTRAL OREGON

BARBARA TRICARICO

SCHIFFER PUBLISHING
4880 Lower Valley Road • Atglen, PA 19310

Other Schiffer Books by Barbara Tricarico:
Oregon, ISBN 978-0-7643-5946-0
Southern Oregon, ISBN 978-0-7643-5948-4
Oregon Coast, ISBN 978-0-7643-5947-7
Ashland, Oregon Day Trips, ISBN 978-0-7643-5014-6

Library of Congress Control Number: 2019947464

Designed by Molly Shields
Cover photo by Barbara Tricarico
Back cover photos, clockwise from left: Neal R. Thompson, Nick Viani, Barbara Tricarico, Hans Stroo

Type set in BentonSans/Cambria

ISBN: 978-0-7643-5945-3
Printed in China

Published by Schiffer Publishing, Ltd.
4880 Lower Valley Road
Atglen, PA 19310
Phone: (610) 593-1777; Fax: (610) 593-2002
E-mail: Info@schifferbooks.com
Web: www.schifferbooks.com

INTRODUCTION

Central Oregon has something for everyone, all four seasons of the year. The Deschutes River provides recreational activities for Bend and Sunriver during the summer. Winter brings snow to central Oregon, drawing skiers to Mount Bachelor and other ski resorts.

The Newberry National Volcanic Monument has more than 54,000 acres of lakes and lava flows. A visit to the High Desert Museum will offer diverse wildlife, culture, art, and natural resources.

The expansive Ochoco National Forest has a number of campgrounds that draw hikers and bikers. If you're lucky, you might even see wild horses! One of the Seven Wonders of Oregon, Smith Rock State Park is a sight to behold with its jagged peaks and red canyon walls.

Bend, one of the fastest growing cities in America, is central Oregon's largest city and is famous for its craft beer. The little town of Sisters (population 2,573) graciously opens its doors to festivals that draw tens of thousands of visitors yearly from all over the world. The town is framed by the picturesque Three Sisters Mountains, popular for hiking and climbing.

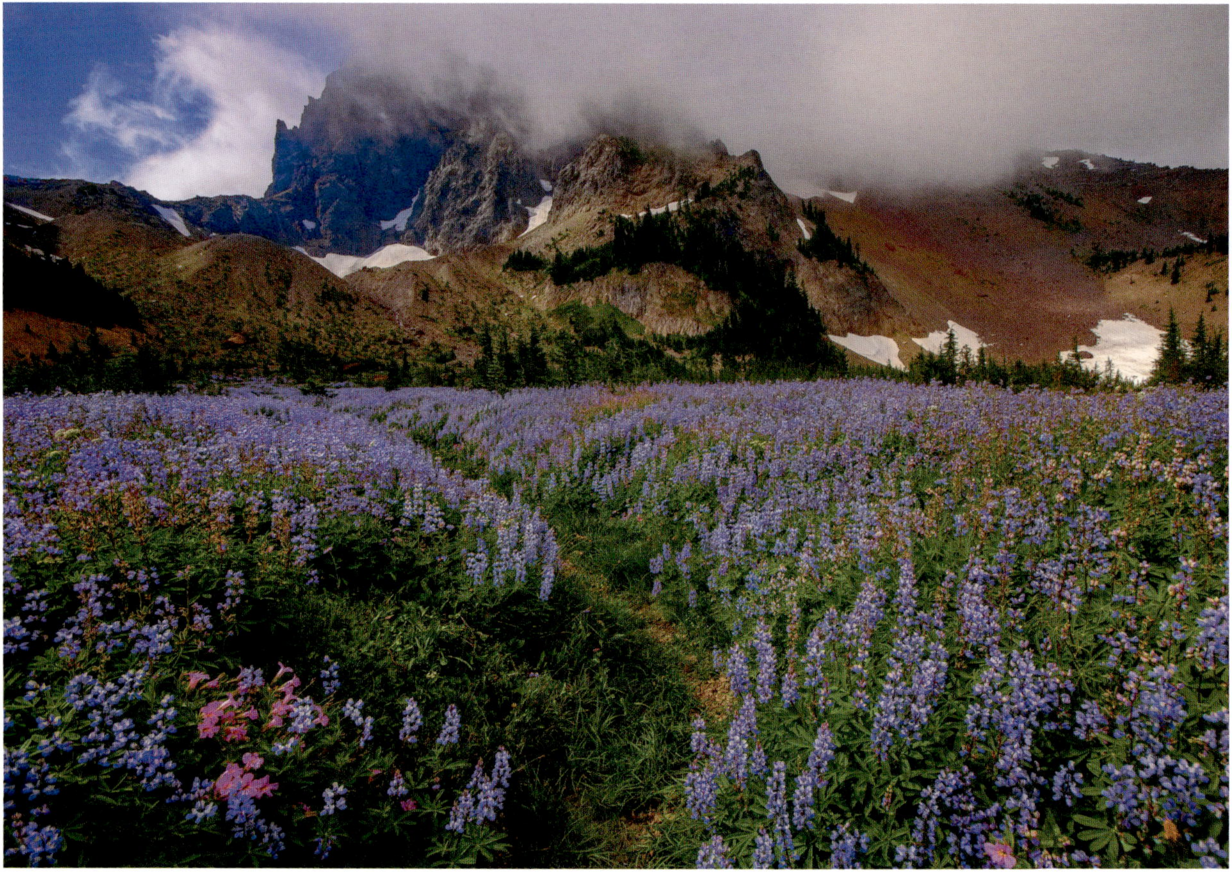

Meadow near Three Finger Jack. Named for an outlaw in the Old West, this area in the Cascade Range is an inactive, glaciated volcano. *Photo by Clem Paslack*.

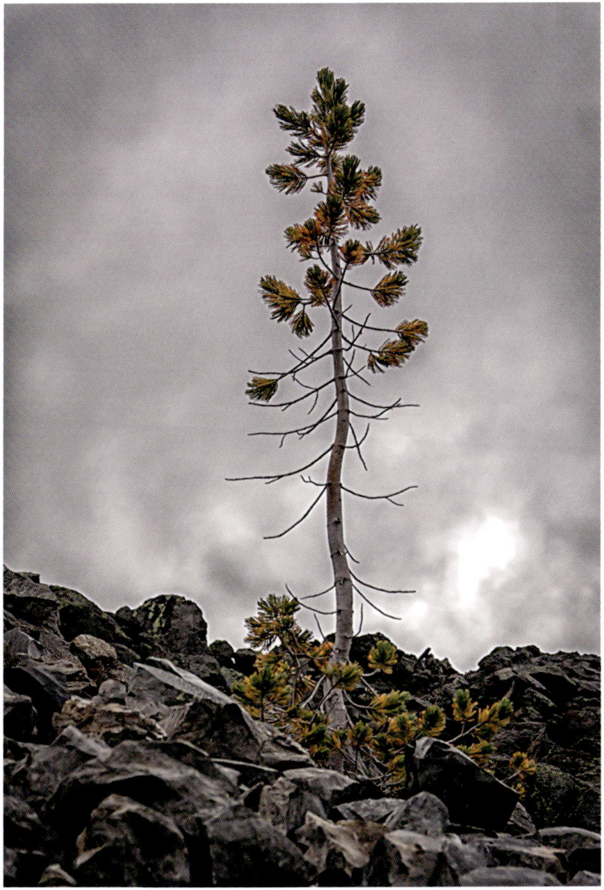

Growth out of the lava, Newberry National Volcanic Monument. *Photo by Barbara Tricarico.*

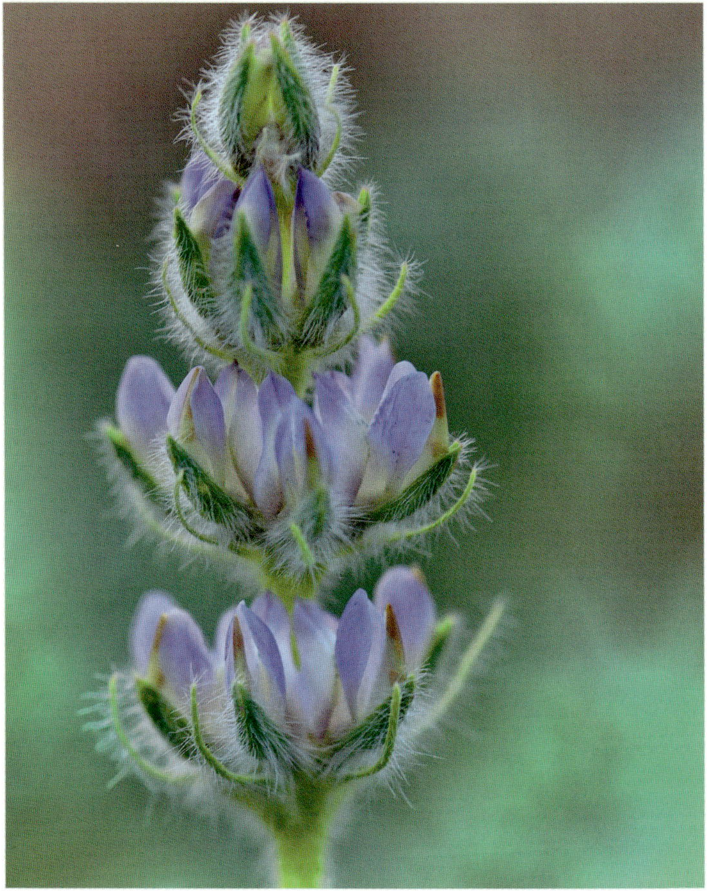

 Wild lupine at Crooked River. *Photo by John Christer Petersen.*

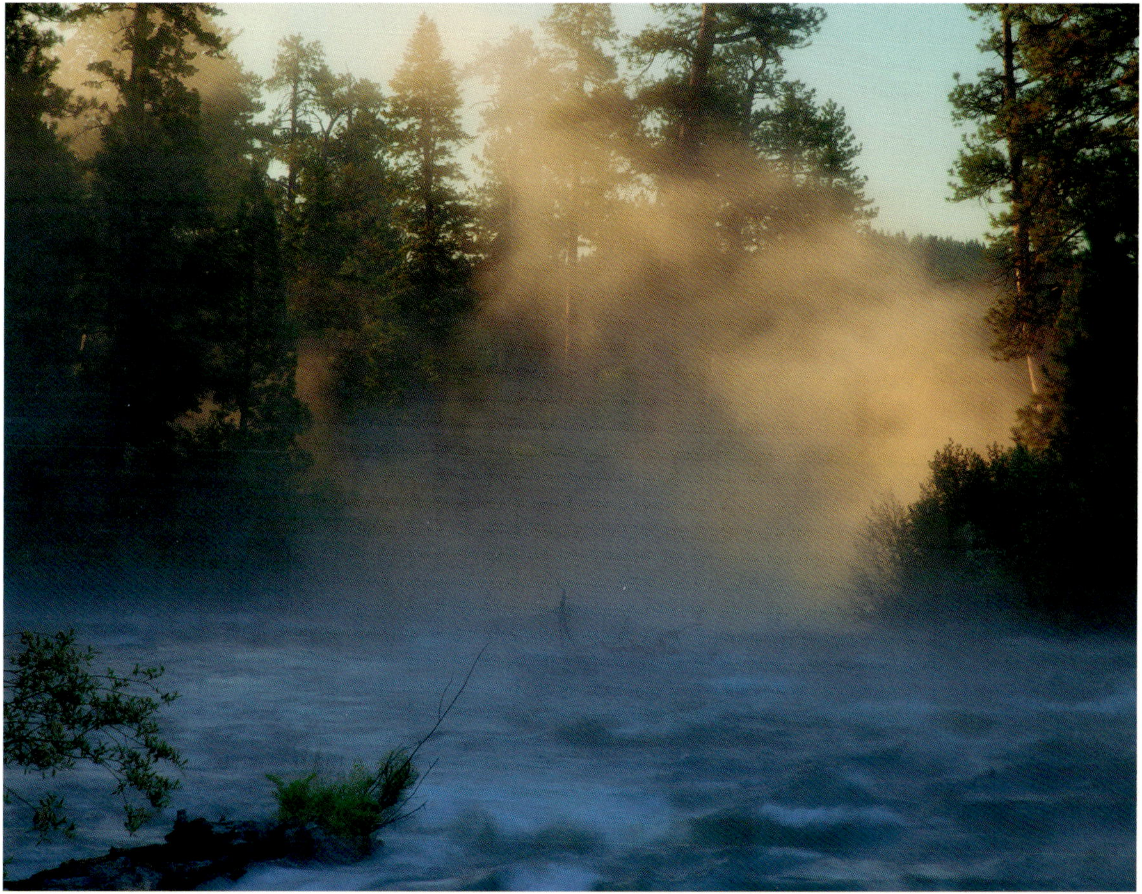

Early dawn, Deschutes River. *Photo by John Christer Petersen.*

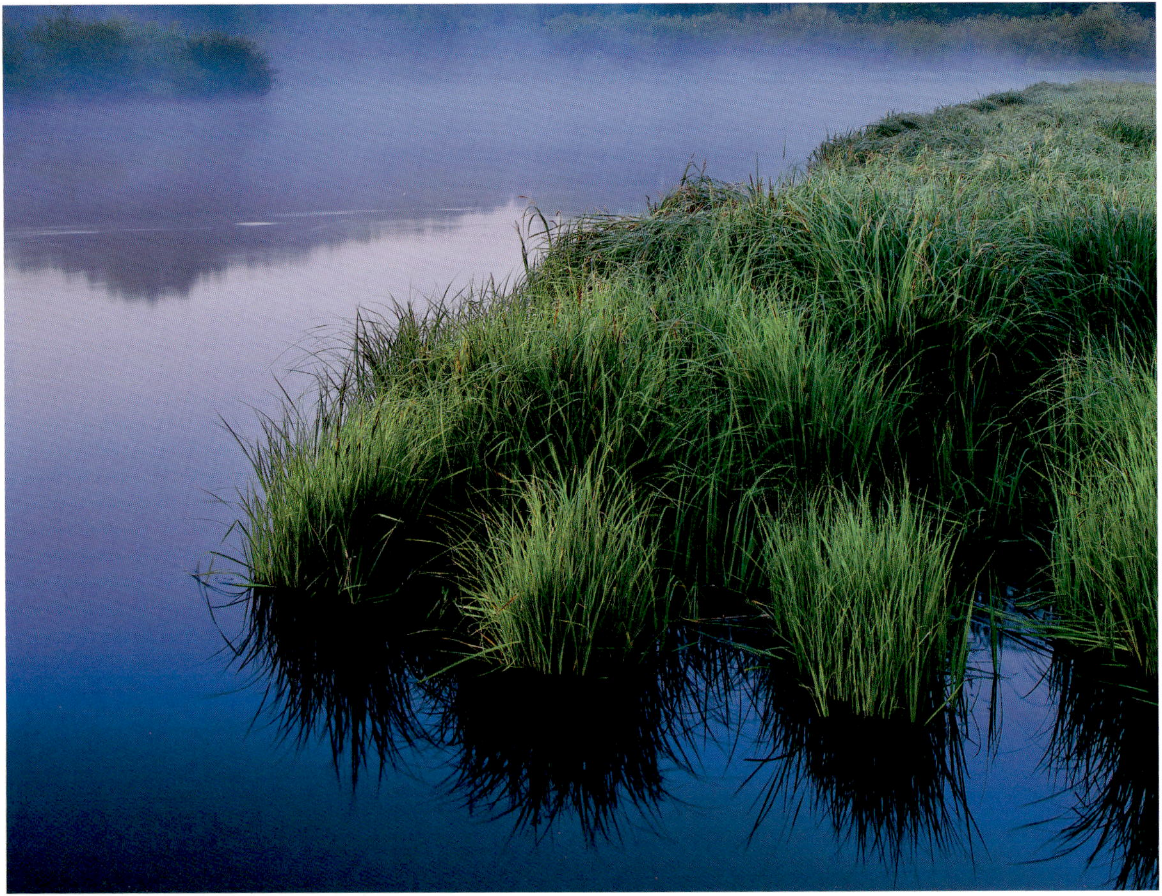

Serenity on the Deschutes River. *Photo by John Christer Petersen.*

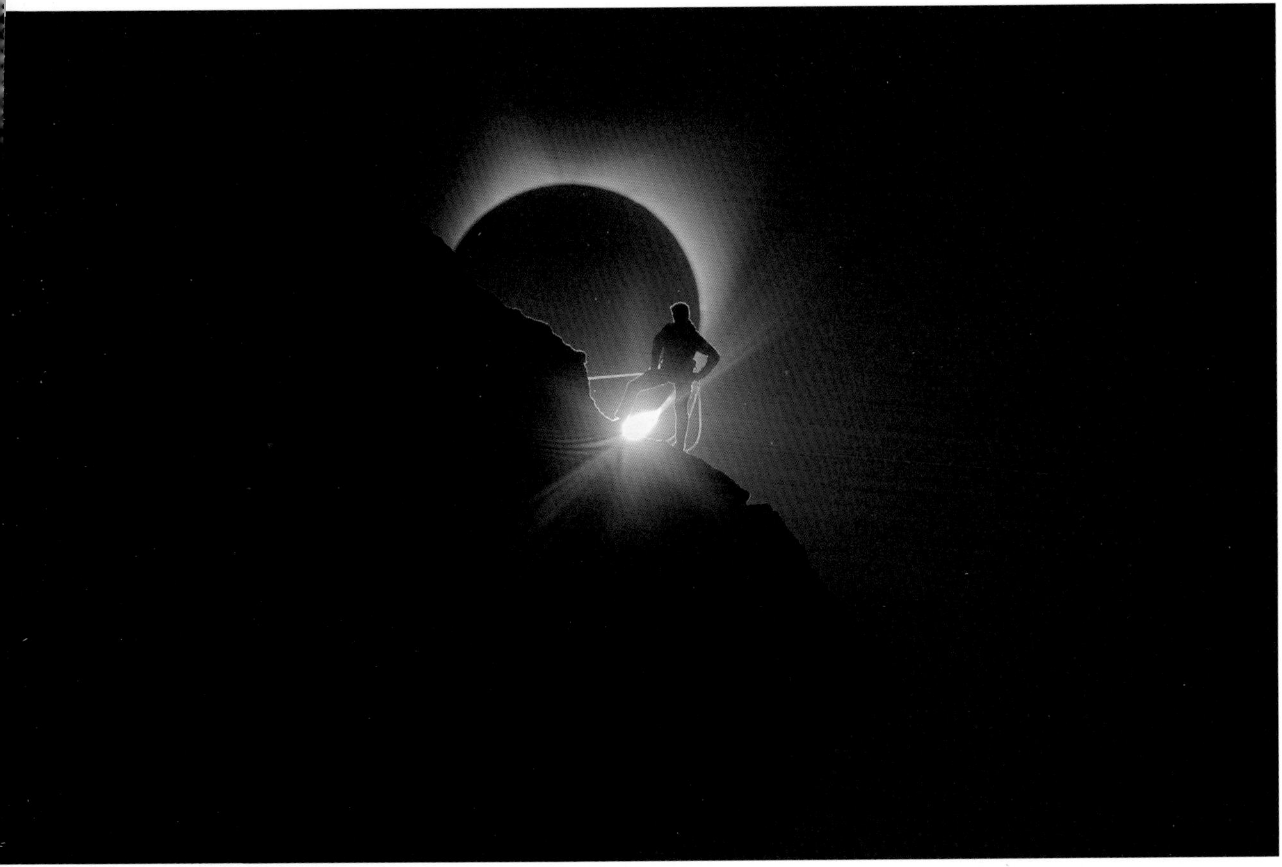

Total solar eclipse. Rock climber Tommy Smith was dramatically captured against a total eclipse at Smith Rock State Park on August 21, 2017. The solar event lasted less than two minutes. *Photo by Andrew Studer.*

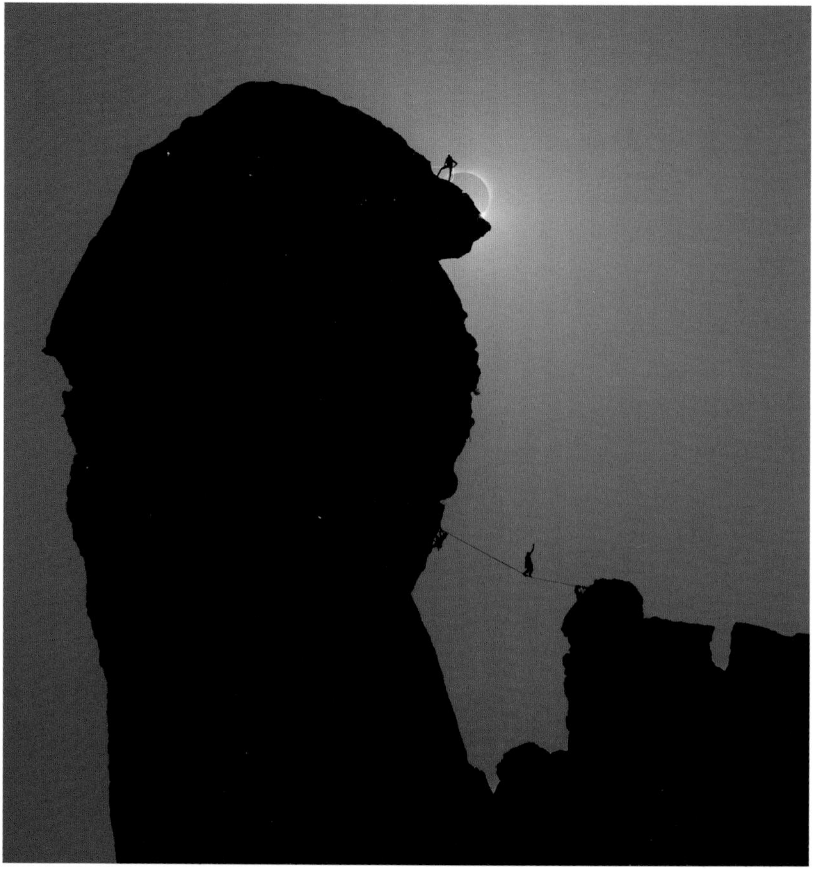

Slackliner Ryan Robinson walks from Springboard into the “mouth” of Monkey Face at Smith Rock State Park, while Tommy Smith poses above. The backdrop is a total solar eclipse that occurred on August 21, 2017. *Photo by Andrew Studer.*

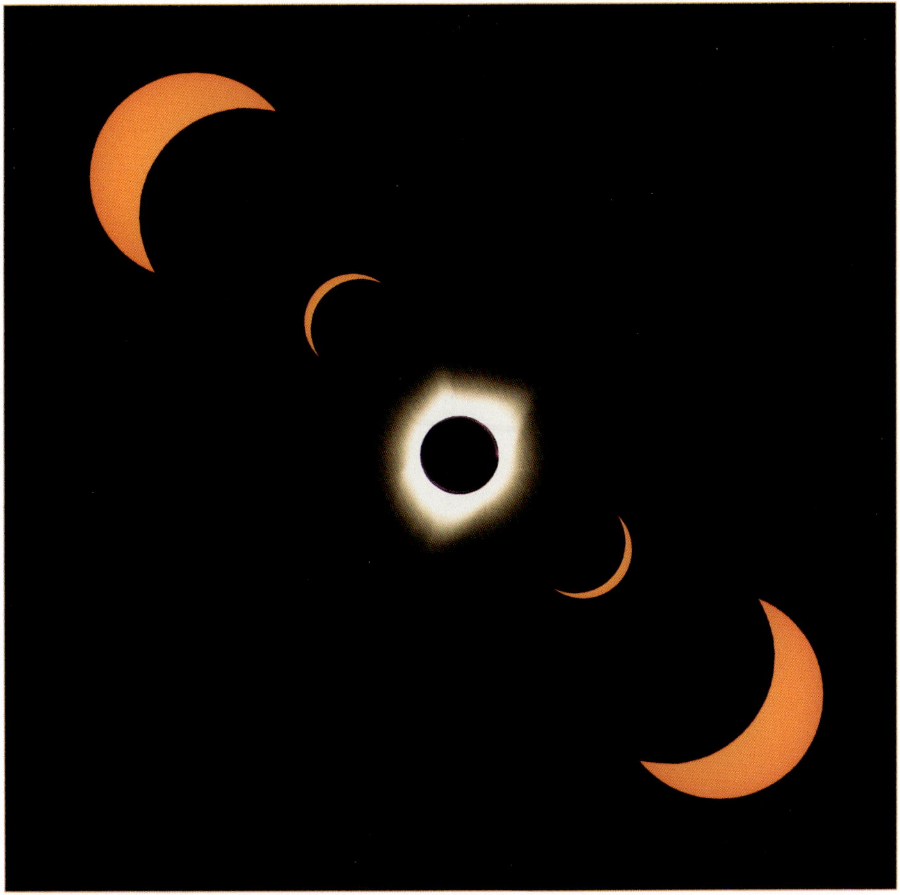

Total solar eclipse composite. *Photo by Alan Ingersoll.*

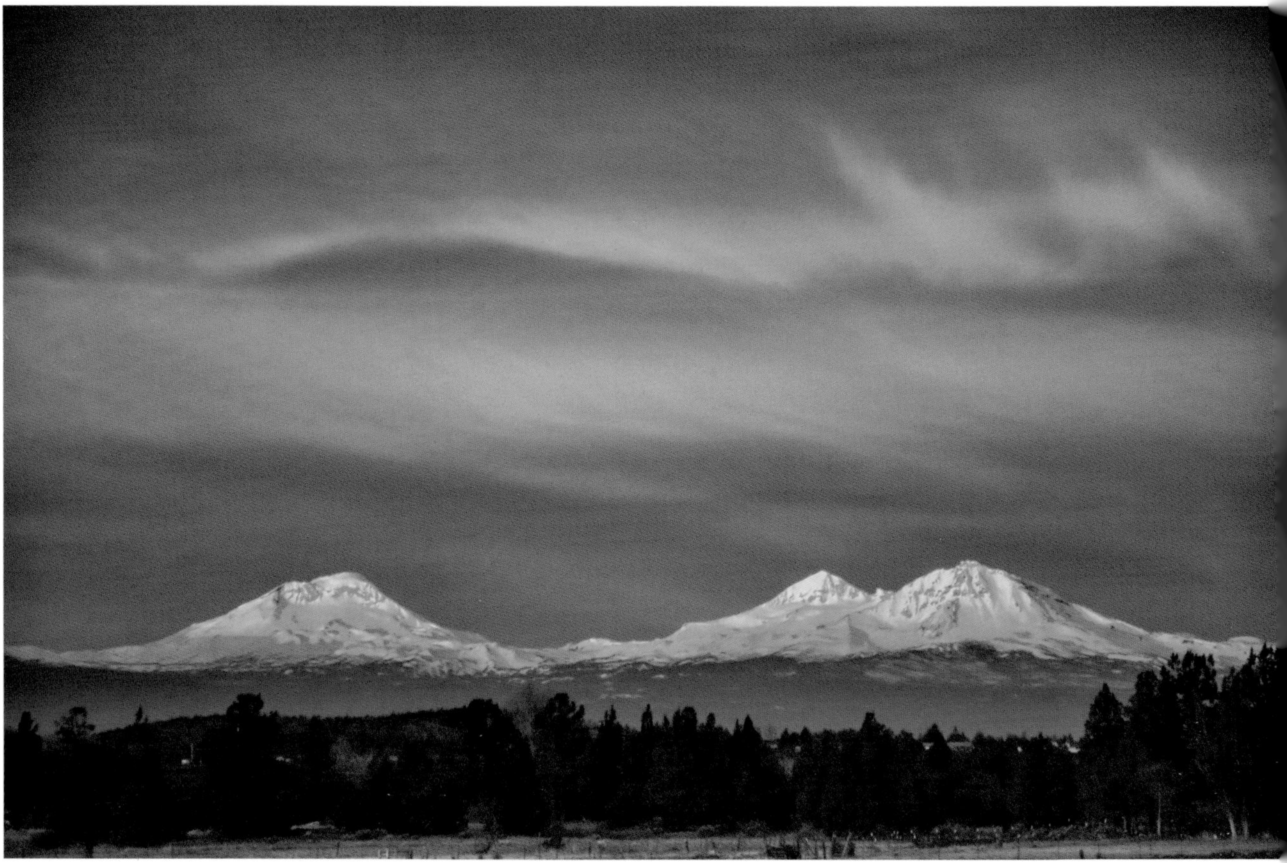

Three Sisters Mountains. Seen for miles around the Sisters area, these volcanic mountains are the third-, fourth-, and fifth-highest peaks in Oregon, at more than 10,000 feet in elevation. *Photo by Hans Stroo.*

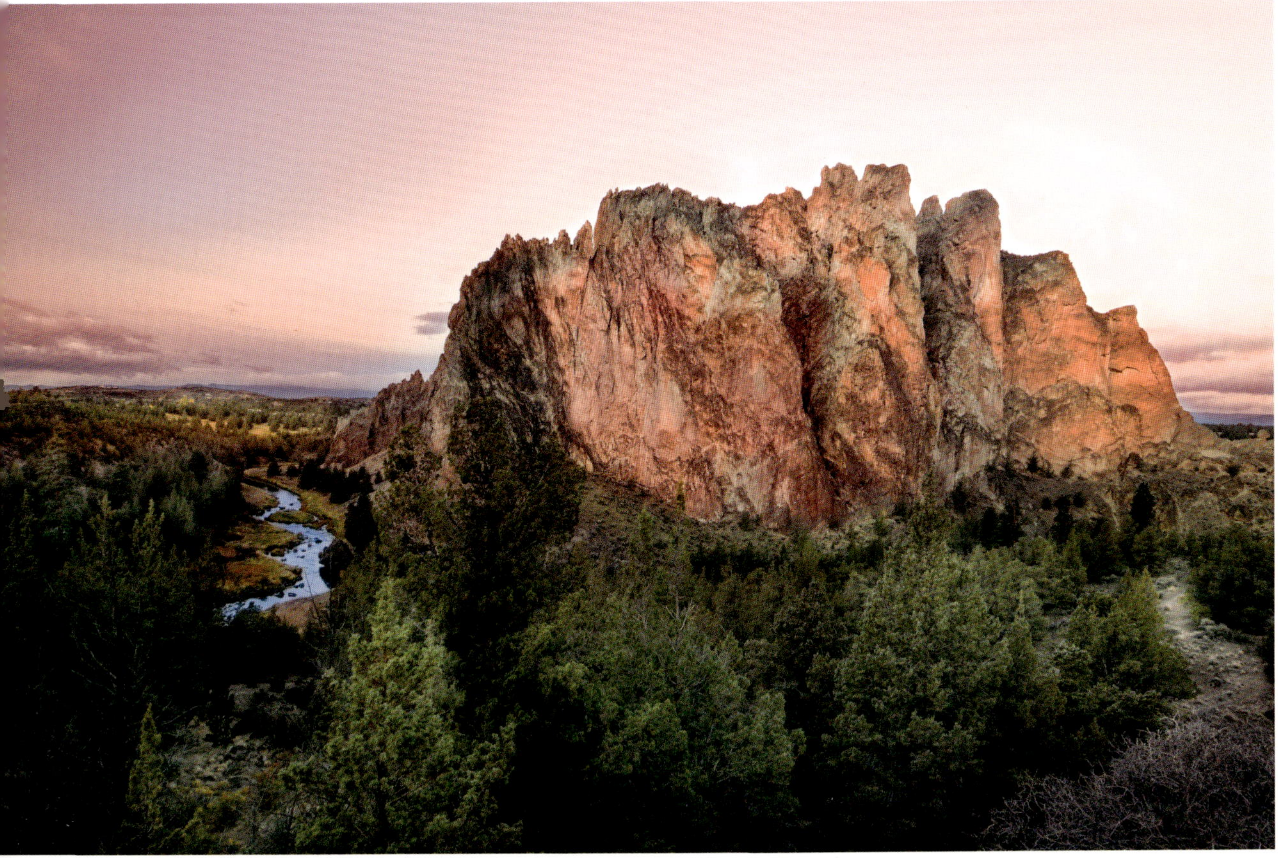

Smith Rock and Crooked River at sunrise. Near the cities of Redmond, Bend, and Sisters, Smith Rock State Park is a popular outdoor destination. *Photo by Barbara Tricarico.*

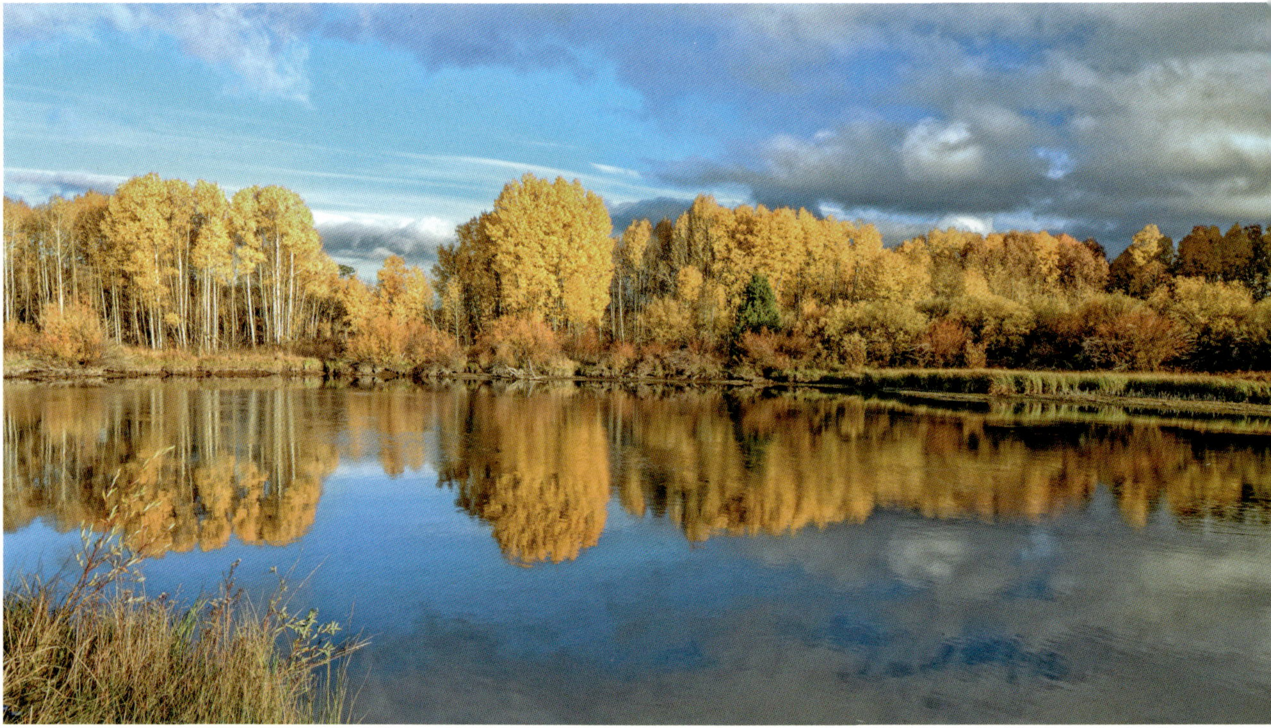

 Deschutes River aspens in Bend. *Photo by Barbara Tricarico.*

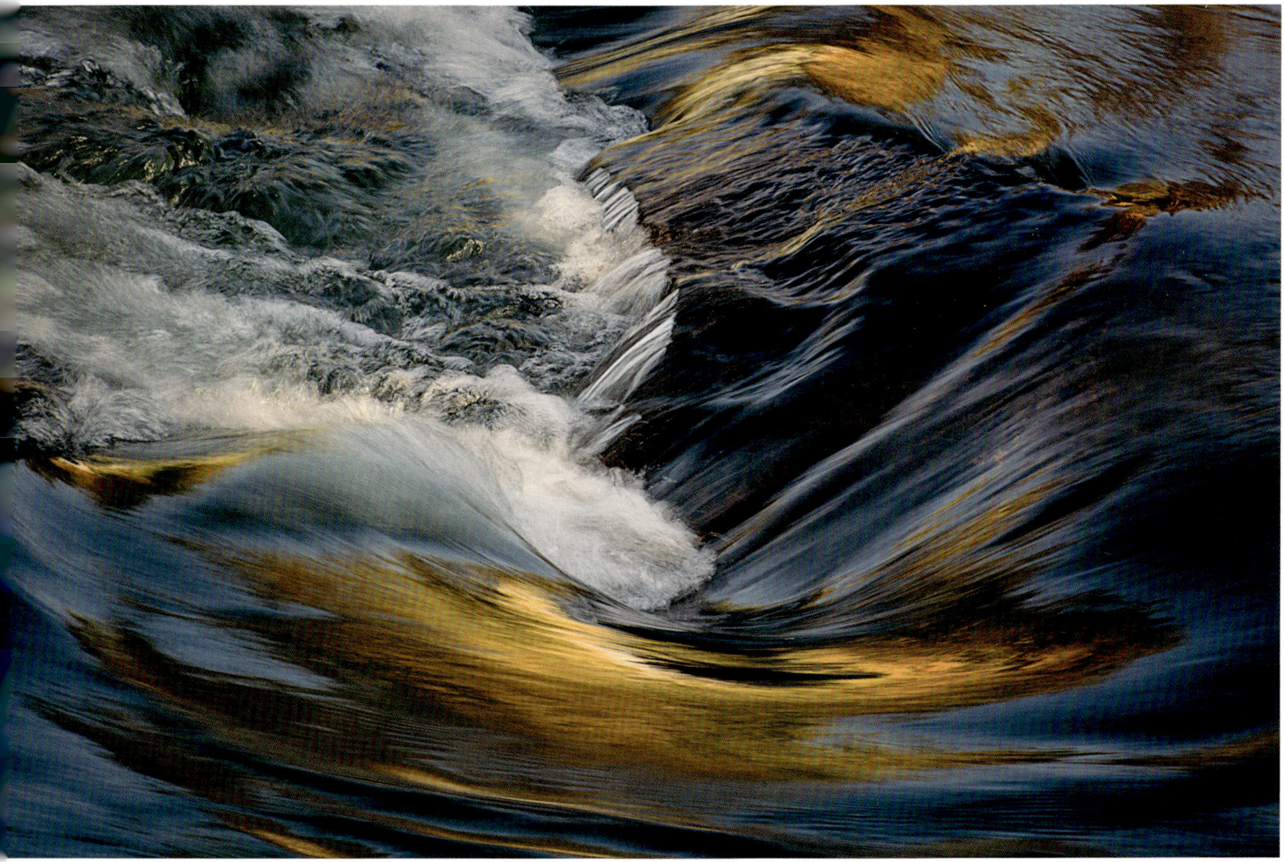

Deschutes River rapids in Bend. *Photo by David Lorenz Winston.*

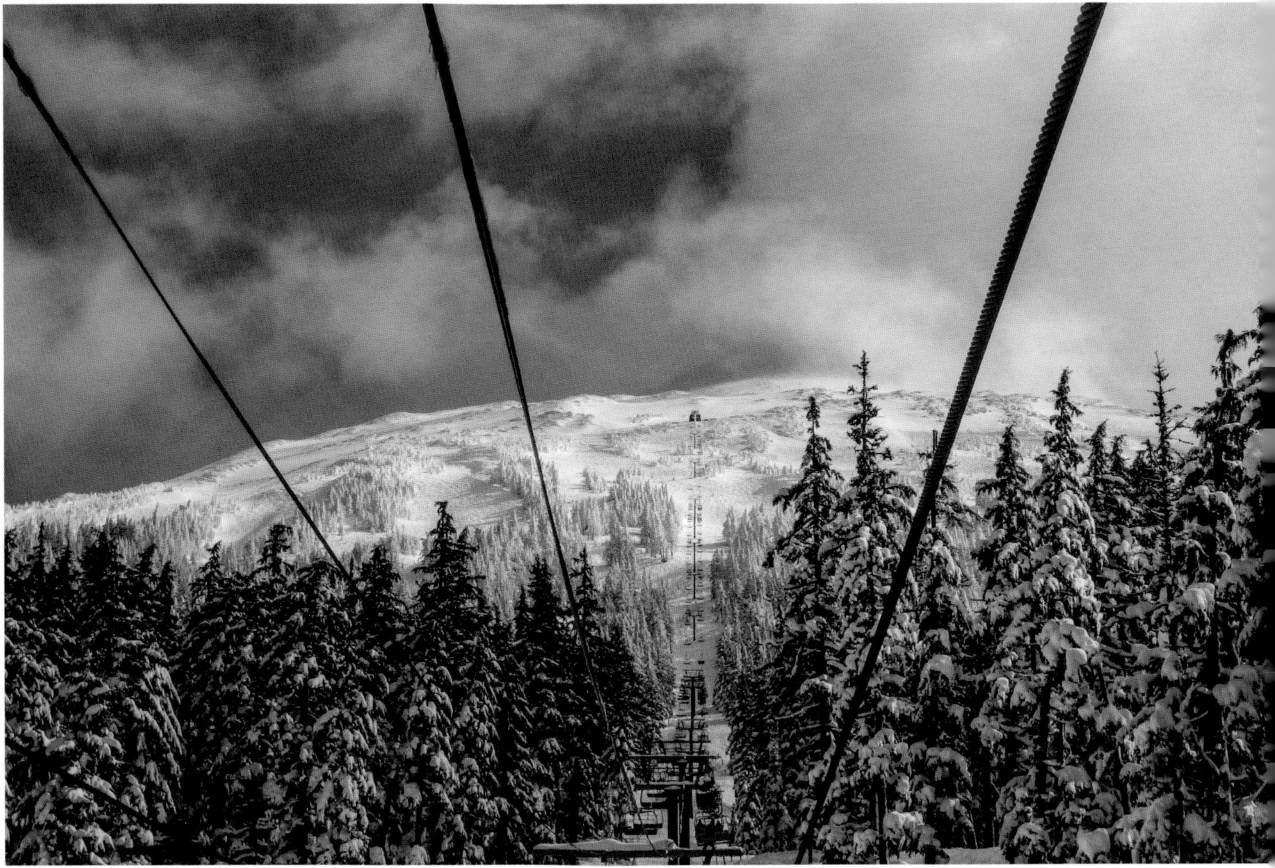

Mount Bachelor ski lift. Located twenty-two miles outside of Bend, the 9,068-foot Mount Bachelor is a popular ski destination with 3,683 acres of skiable area. It is the only Cascade volcano with a chairlift to the summit. *Photo by George F. Peterson.*

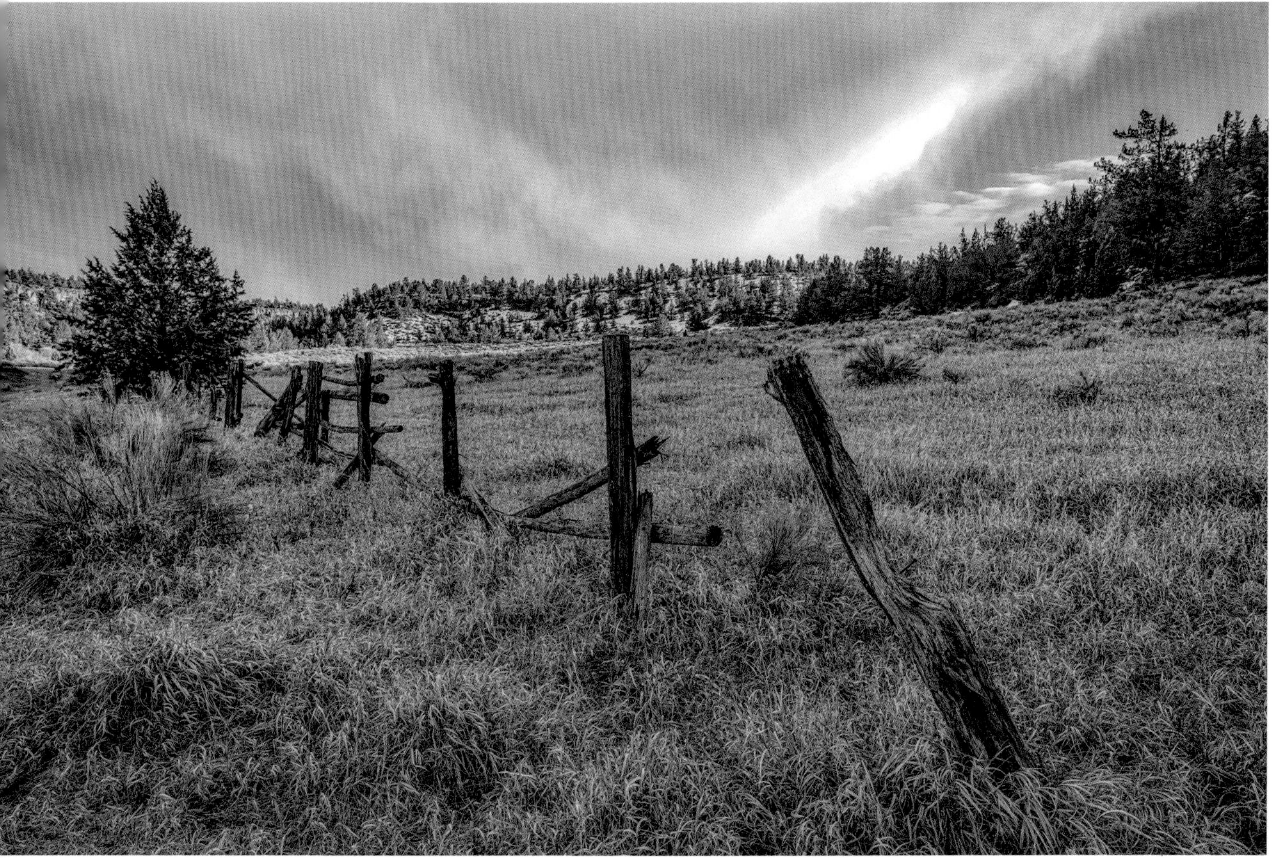

Tumalo. *Photo by Nick Viani.*

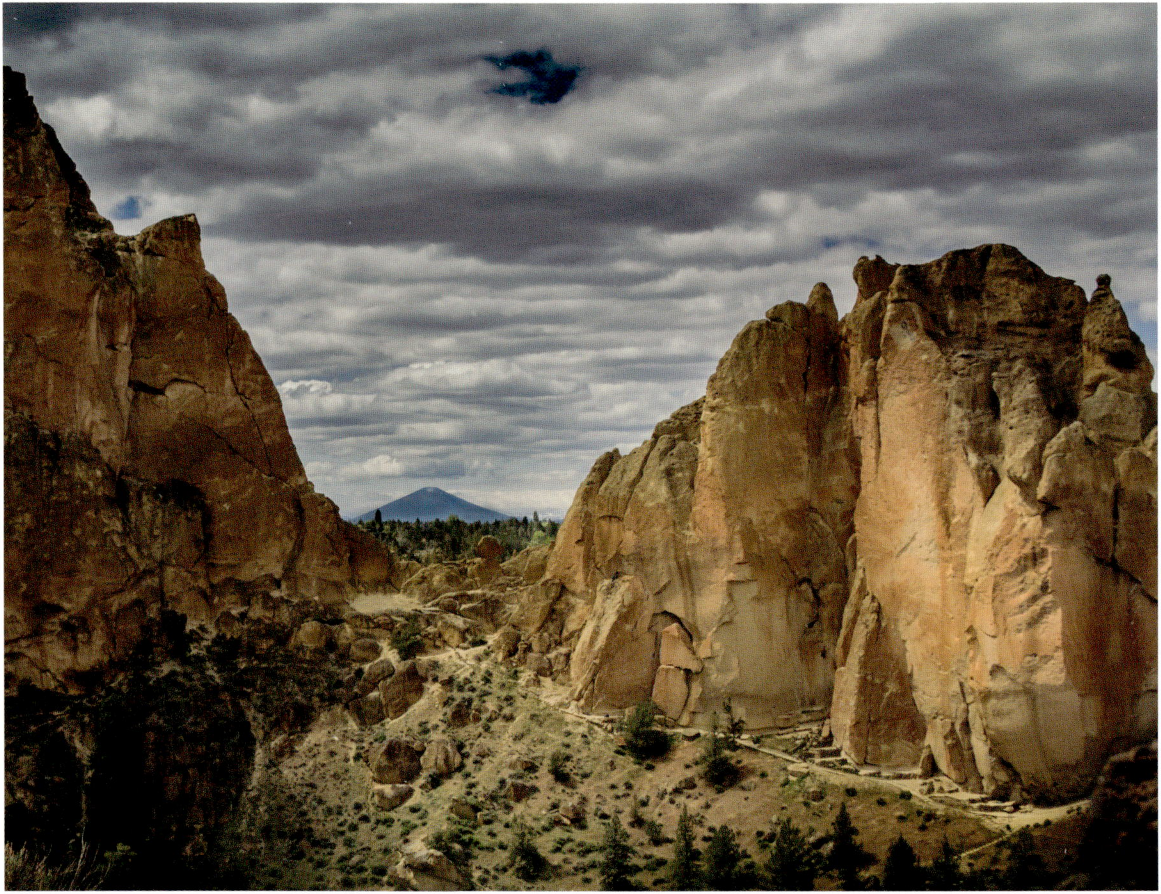

 Smith Rock State Park, with Black Butte in background. *Photo by Judy Benson LaNier.*

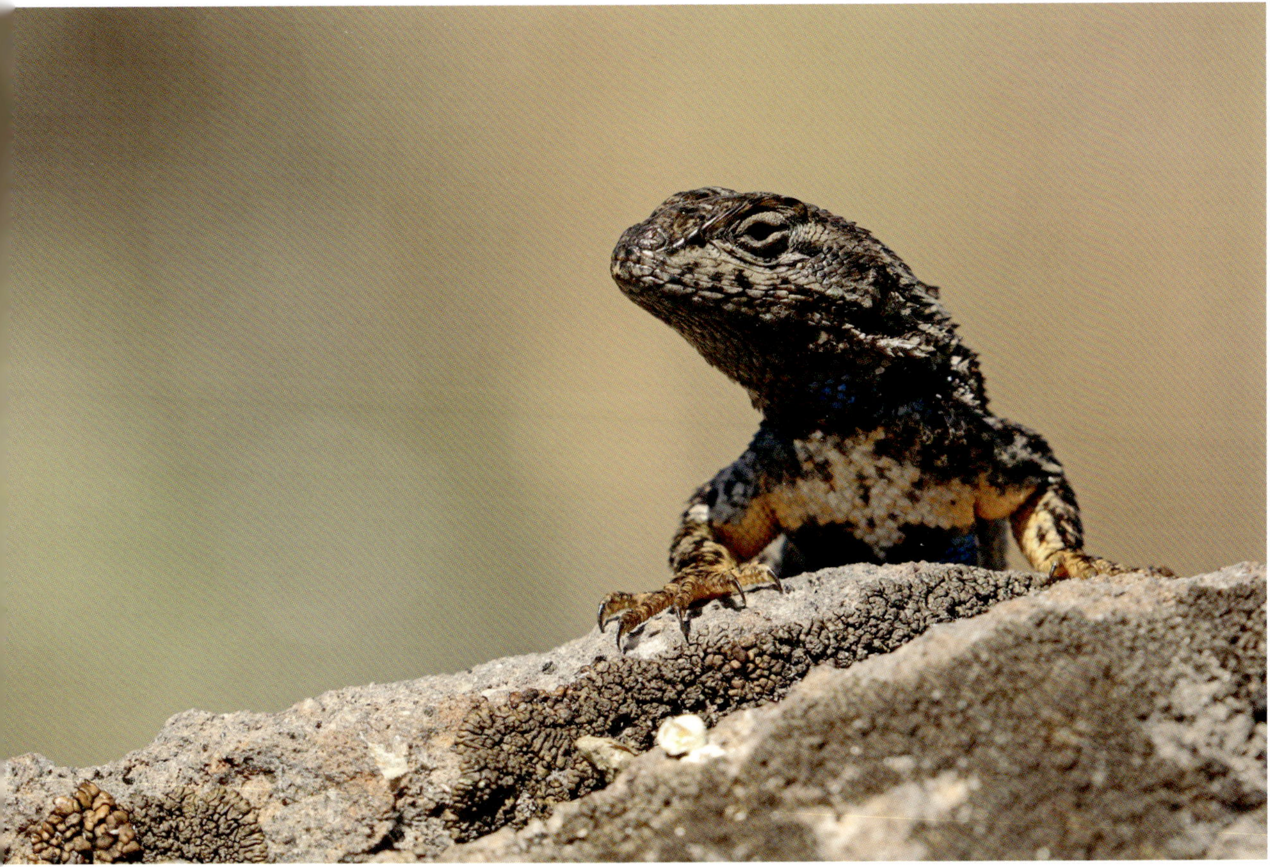

Western fence lizard. *Photo by Dan Elster.*

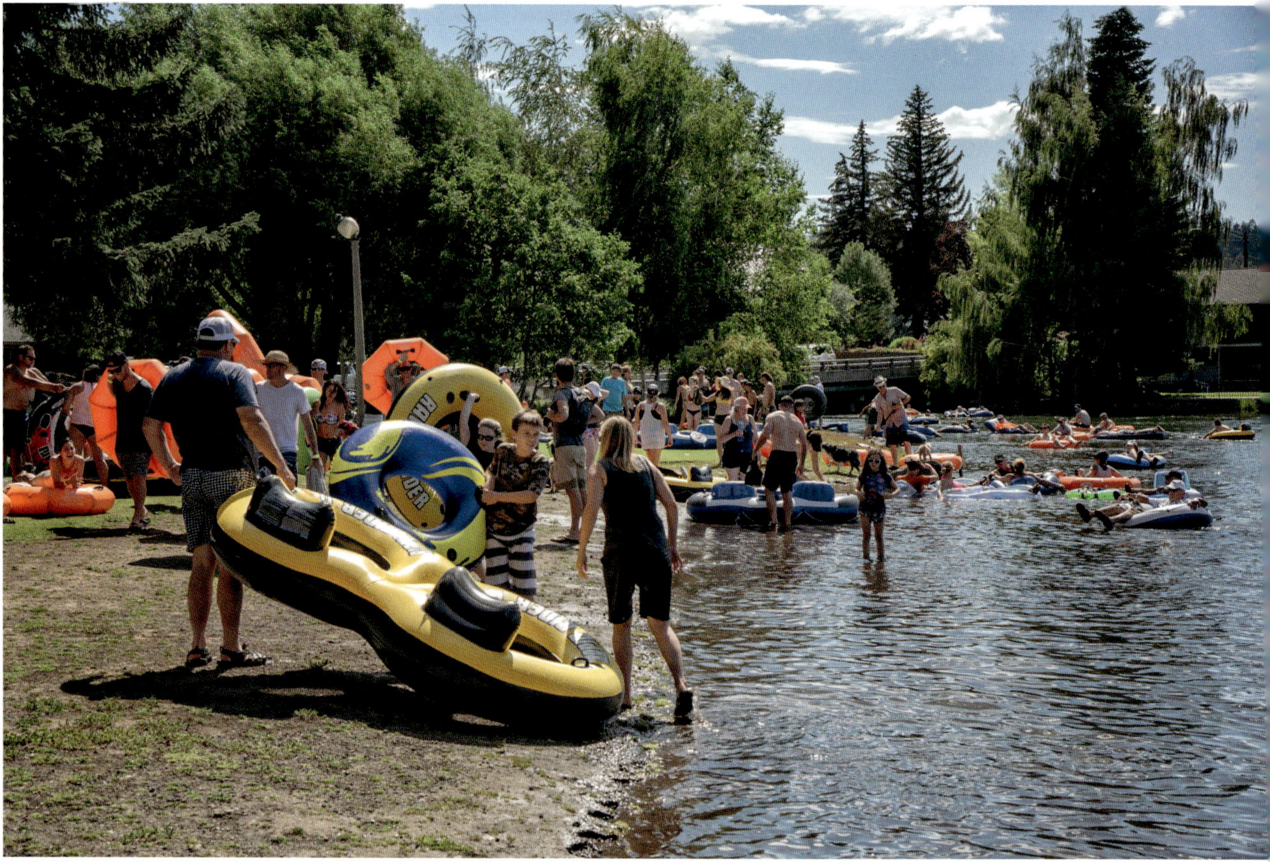

Tubing the Deschutes River is a popular summertime activity at Drake Park in Bend. *Photo by Barbara Tricarico.*

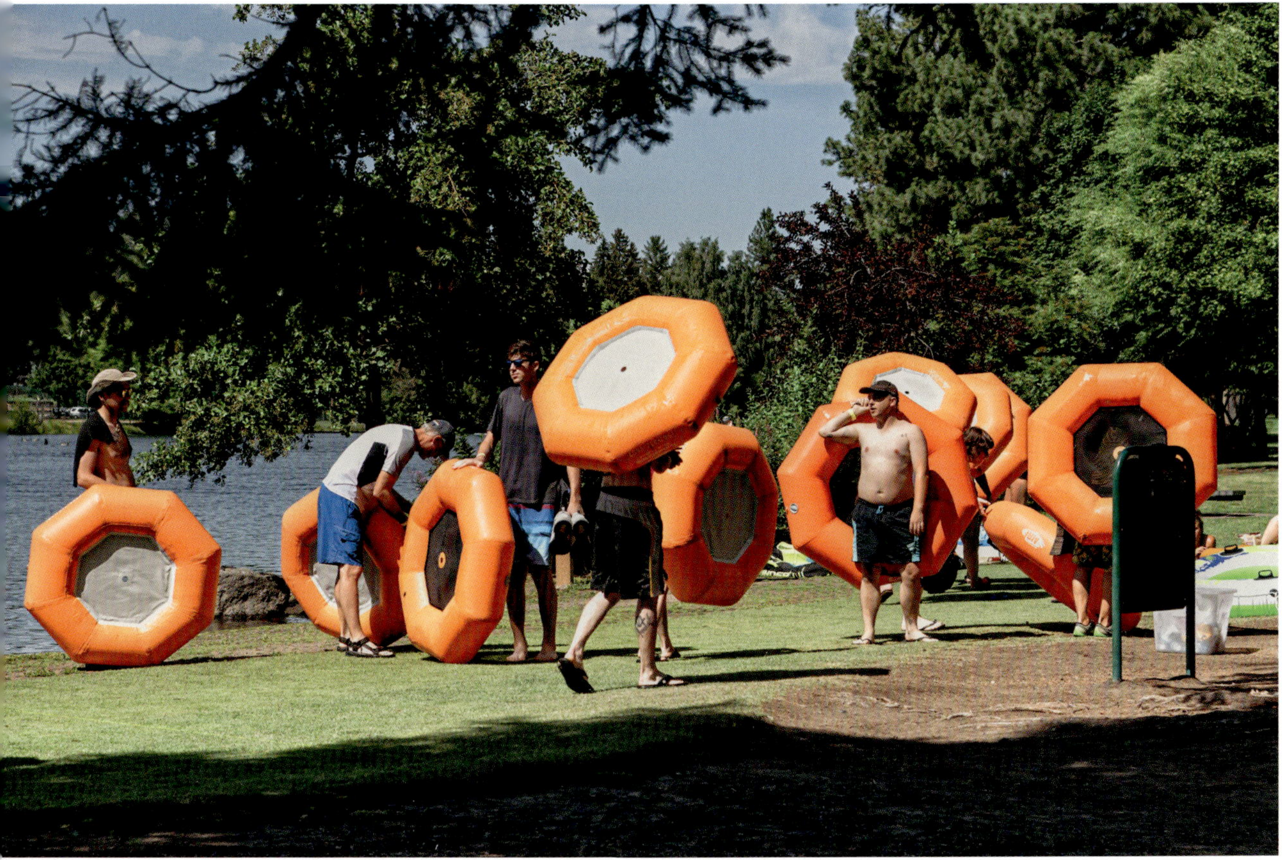

Deschutes River at Drake Park in Bend. *Photo by Barbara Tricarico.*

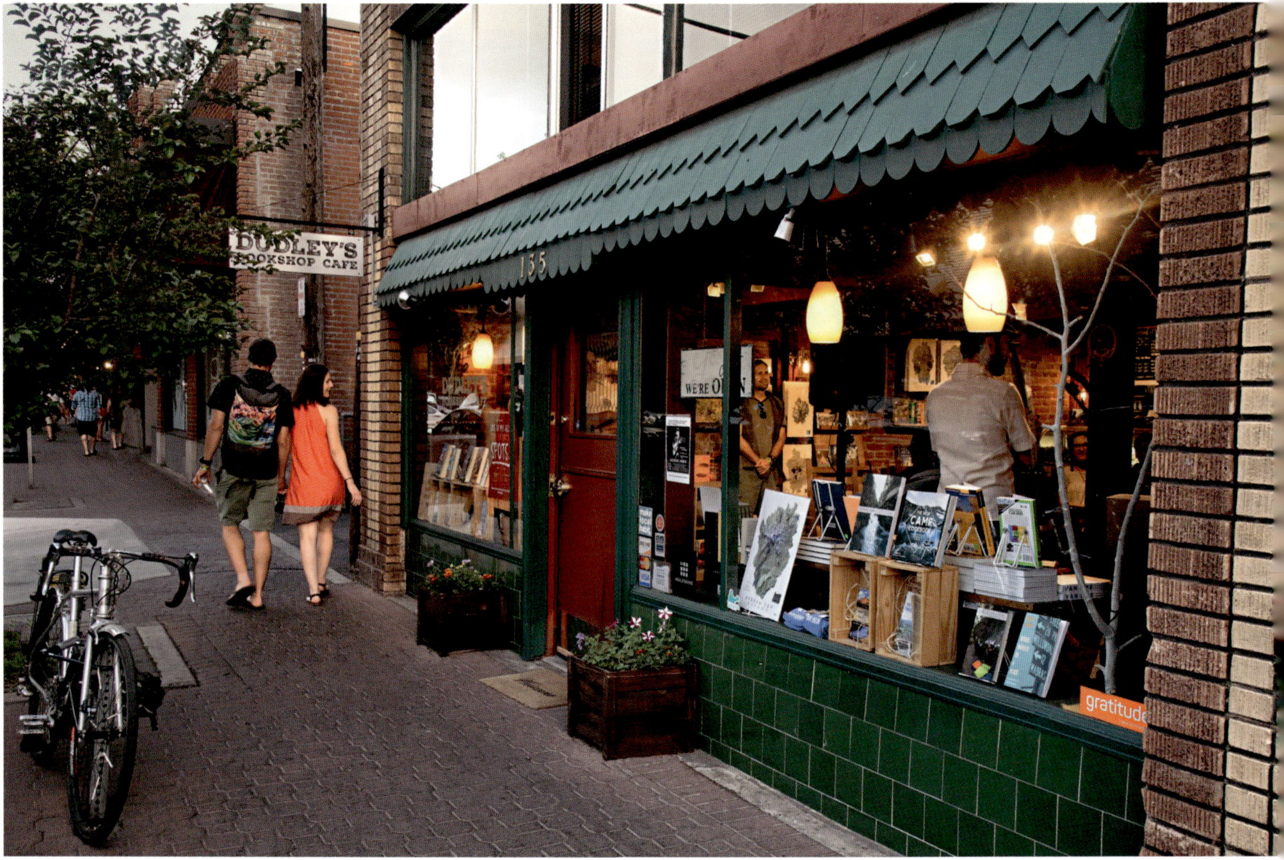

 Strolling in downtown Bend. *Photo by Barbara Tricarico.*

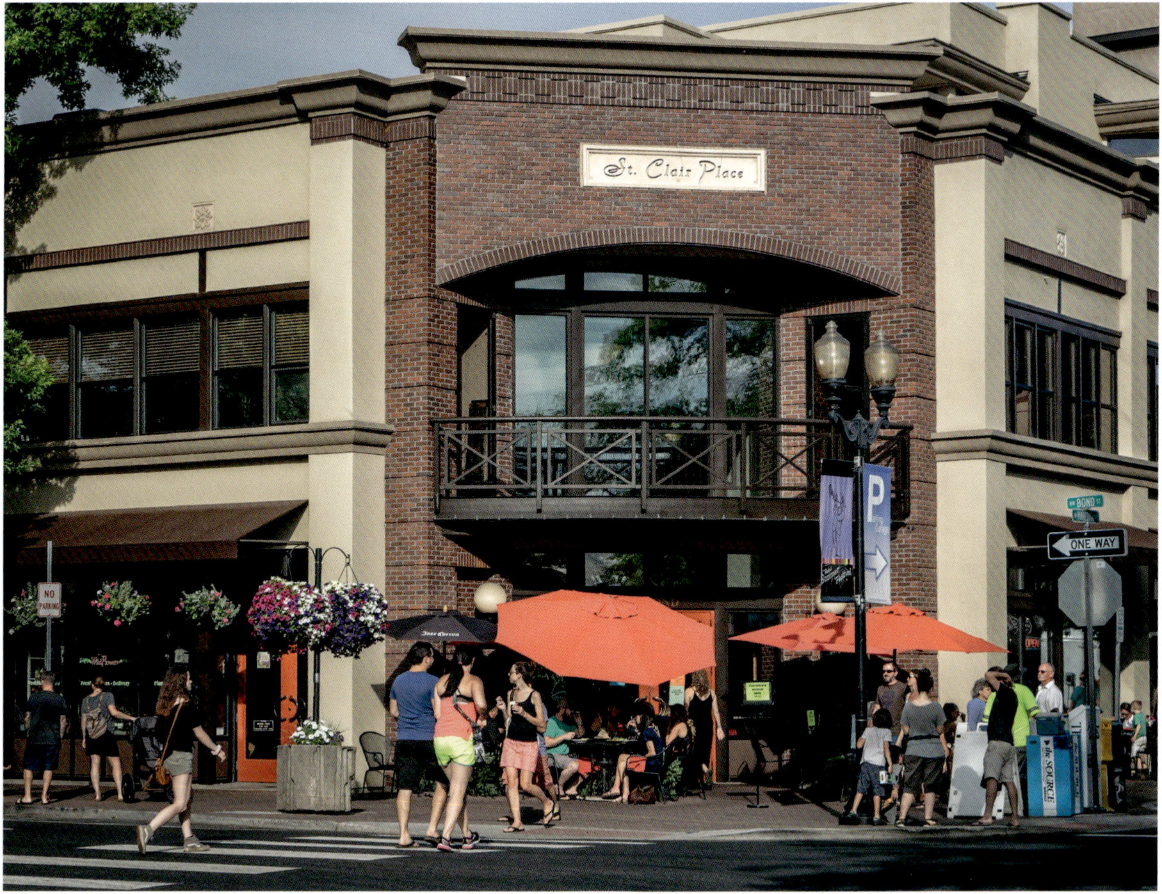

Downtown Bend. *Photo by Barbara Tricarico.*

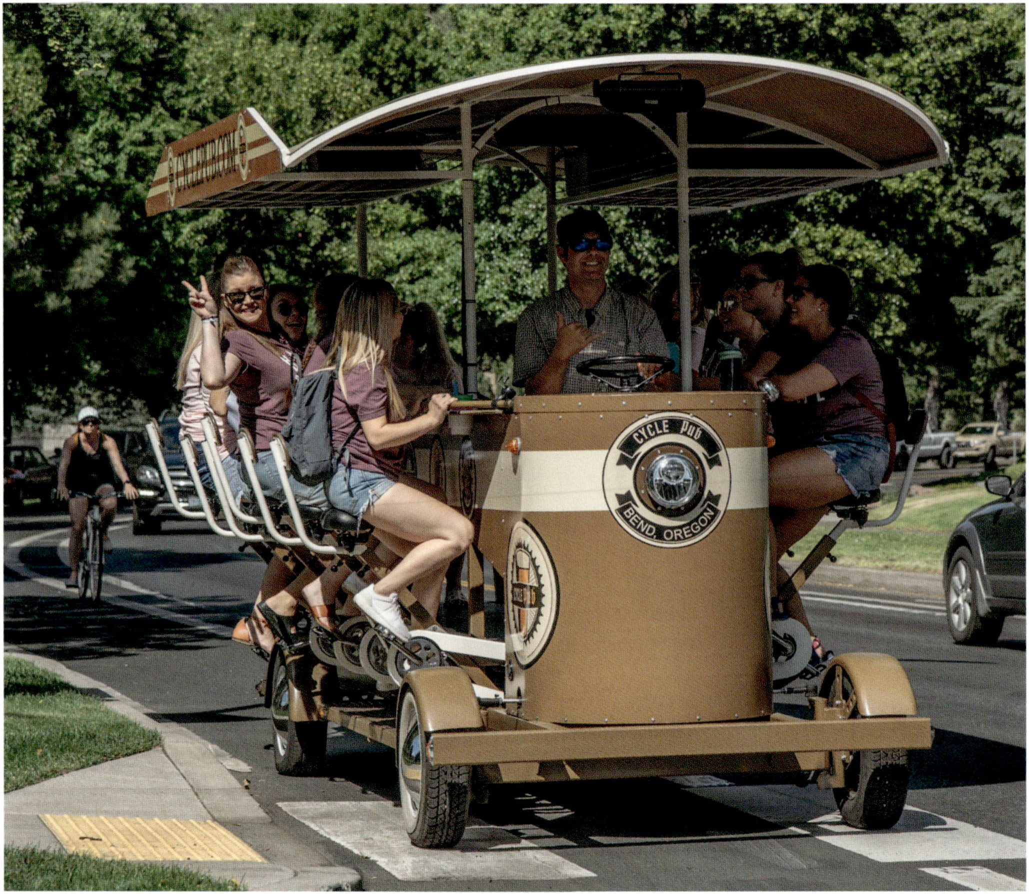

 Rolling pub on wheels. "The Official Bend Ale Trail" features the town's many world-class craft breweries. *Photo by Barbara Tricarico.*

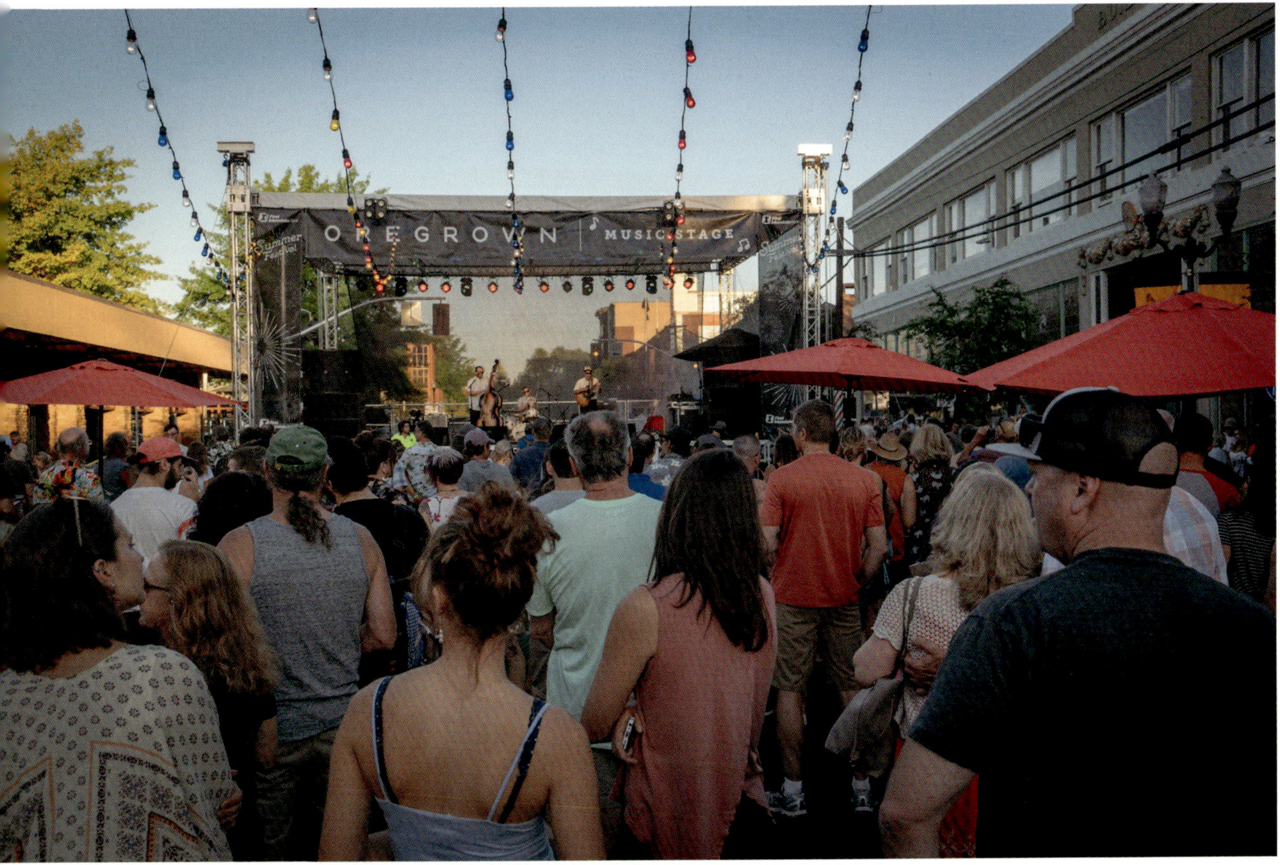

Bend Summer Festival. For more than twenty-eight years, and drawing more than 40,000 people, Bend's streets have opened to live music, fine food, and libations over the course of a long summer weekend. *Photo by Barbara Tricarico.*

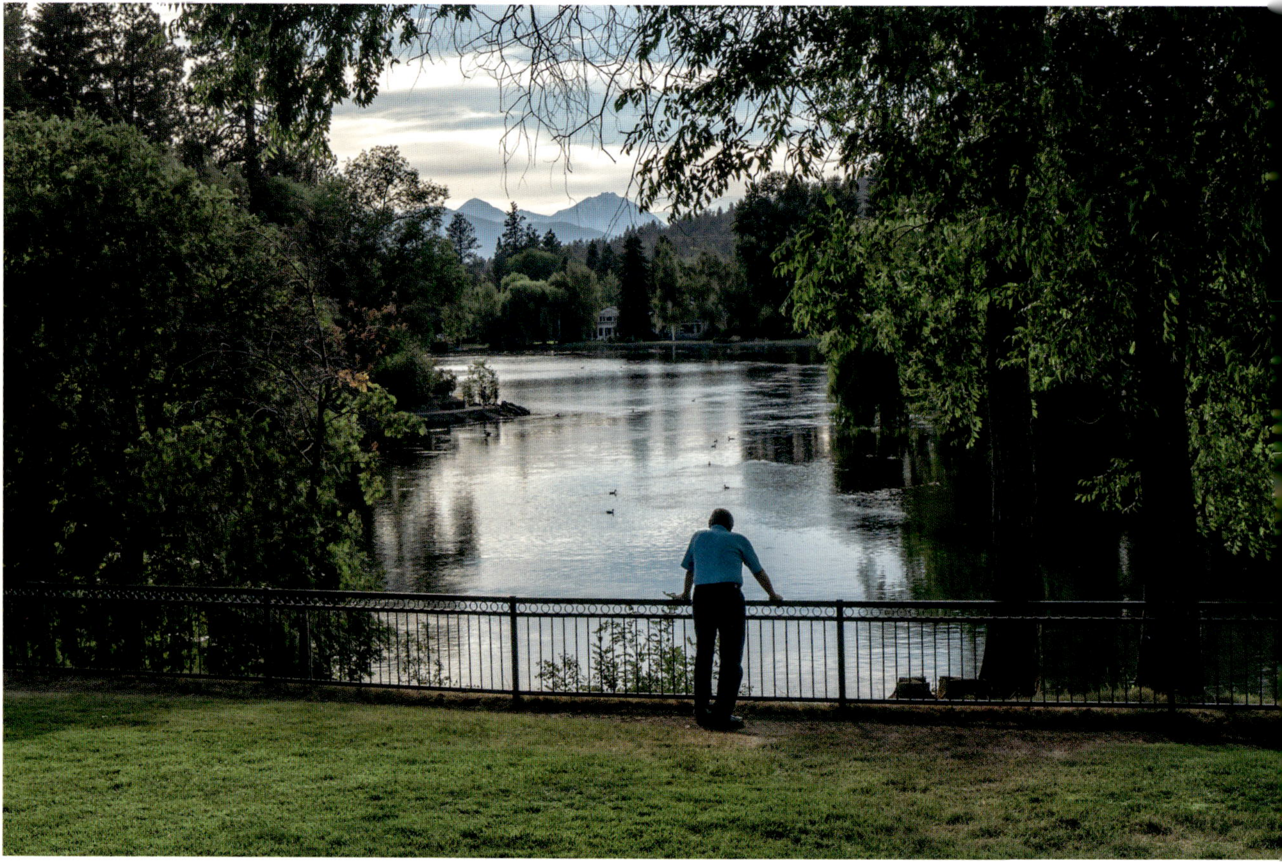

 Mirror Pond, Bend. *Photo by Barbara Tricarico.*

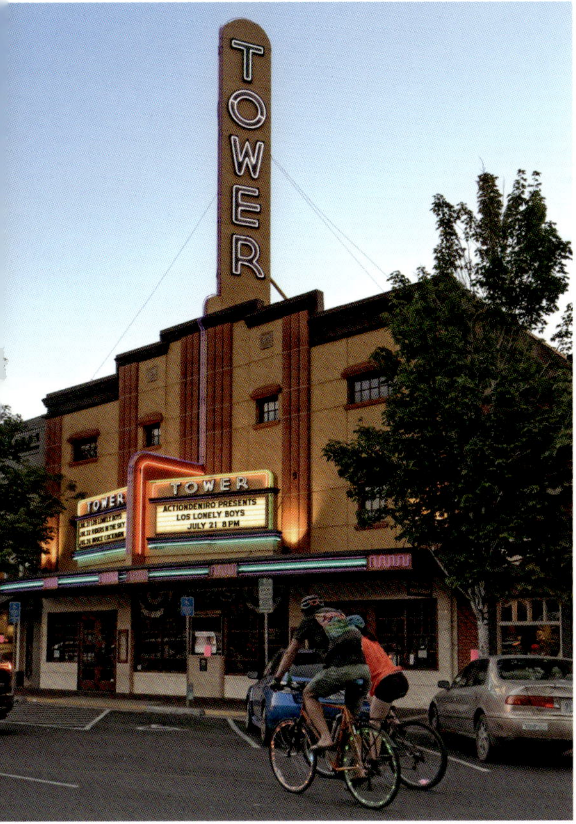

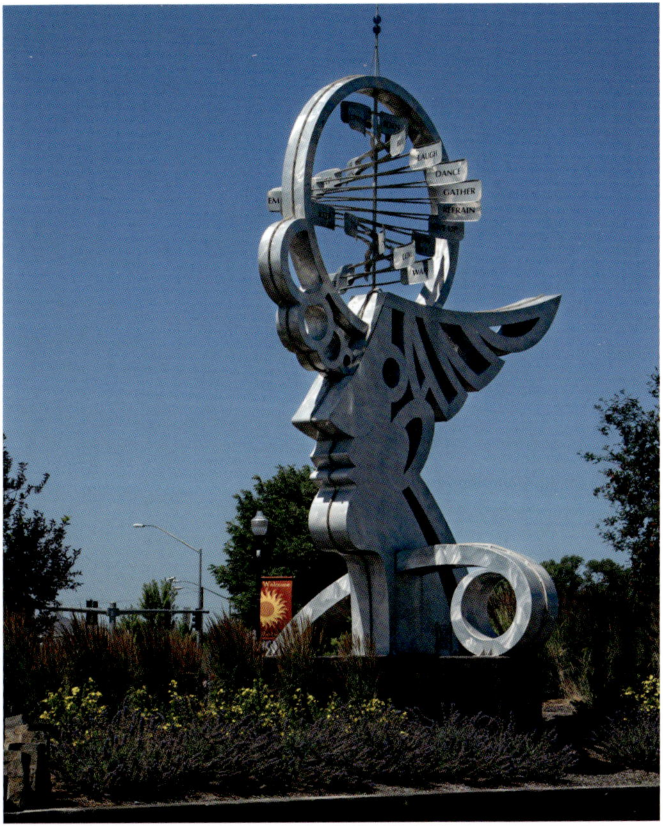

Tower Theatre, Bend. The theater was built in 1940. *Photo by Barbara Tricarico.* • *Thoughts of Flight*, Redmond. Located at the Eastern Y Gateway, the statue depicts Redmond's industrial heritage and was created by local artist Jerry Werner. *Photo by Barbara Tricarico.*

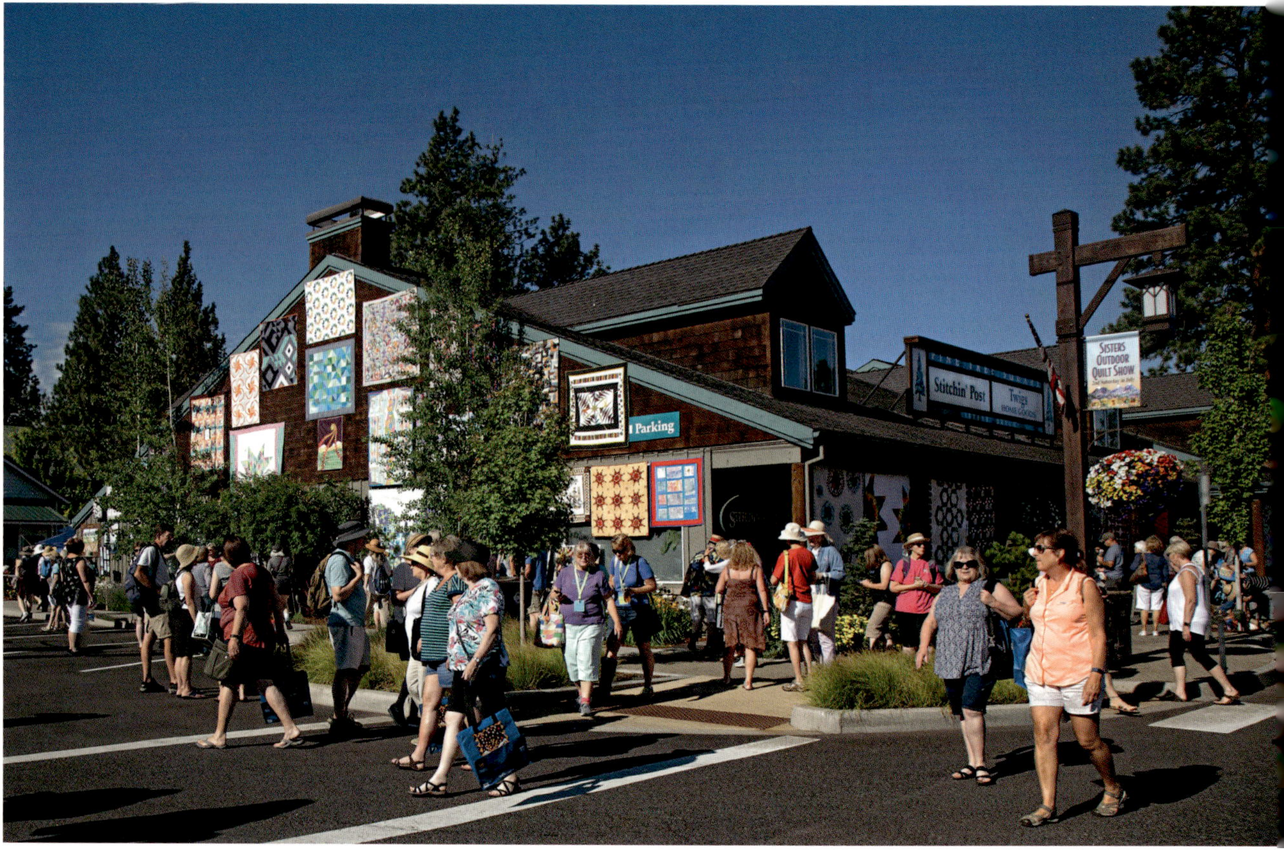

Sisters Outdoor Quilt Show. Since 1975, this annual event has attracted more than 10,000 visitors from all over the world to the small town of Sisters, population 2,500. It is recognized as the world's largest outdoor quilt show and sale, with weeklong classes and workshops. *Photo by Barbara Tricarico.*

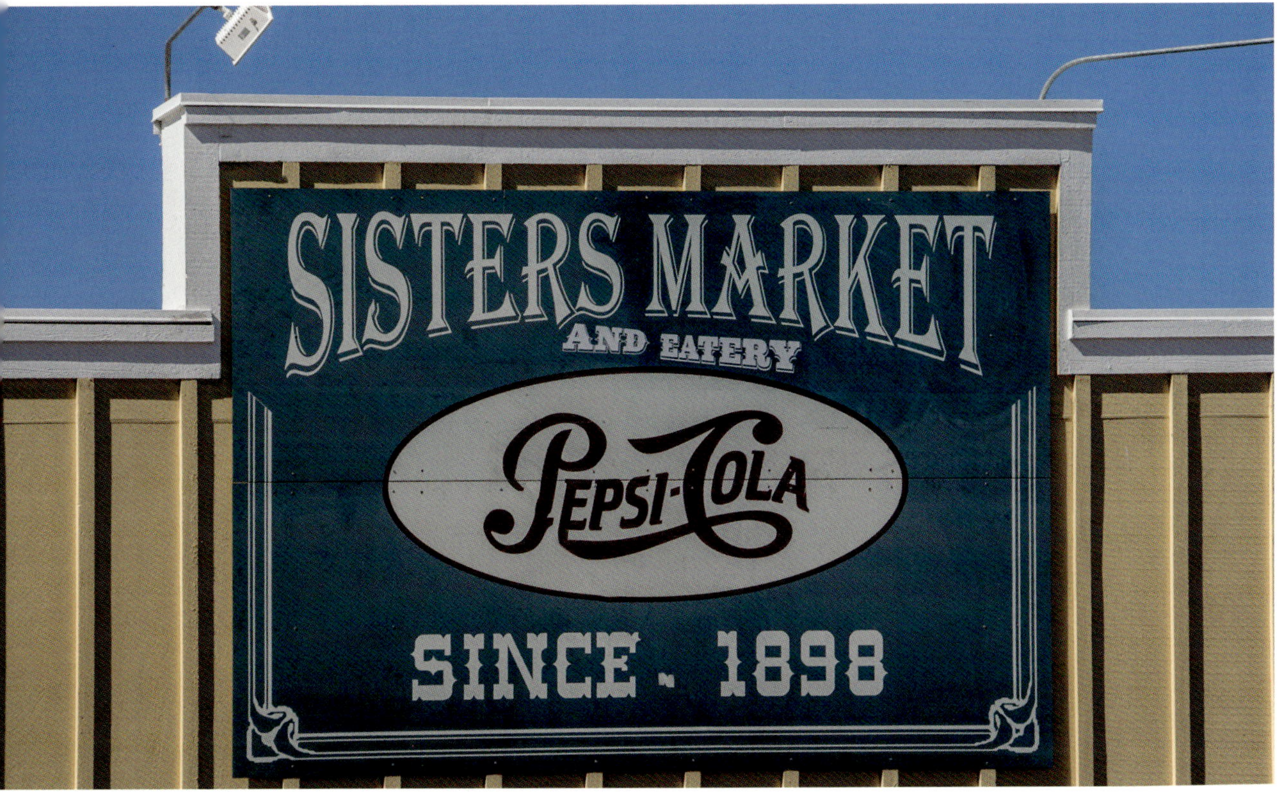

Sisters Market sign. *Photo by George F. Peterson.*

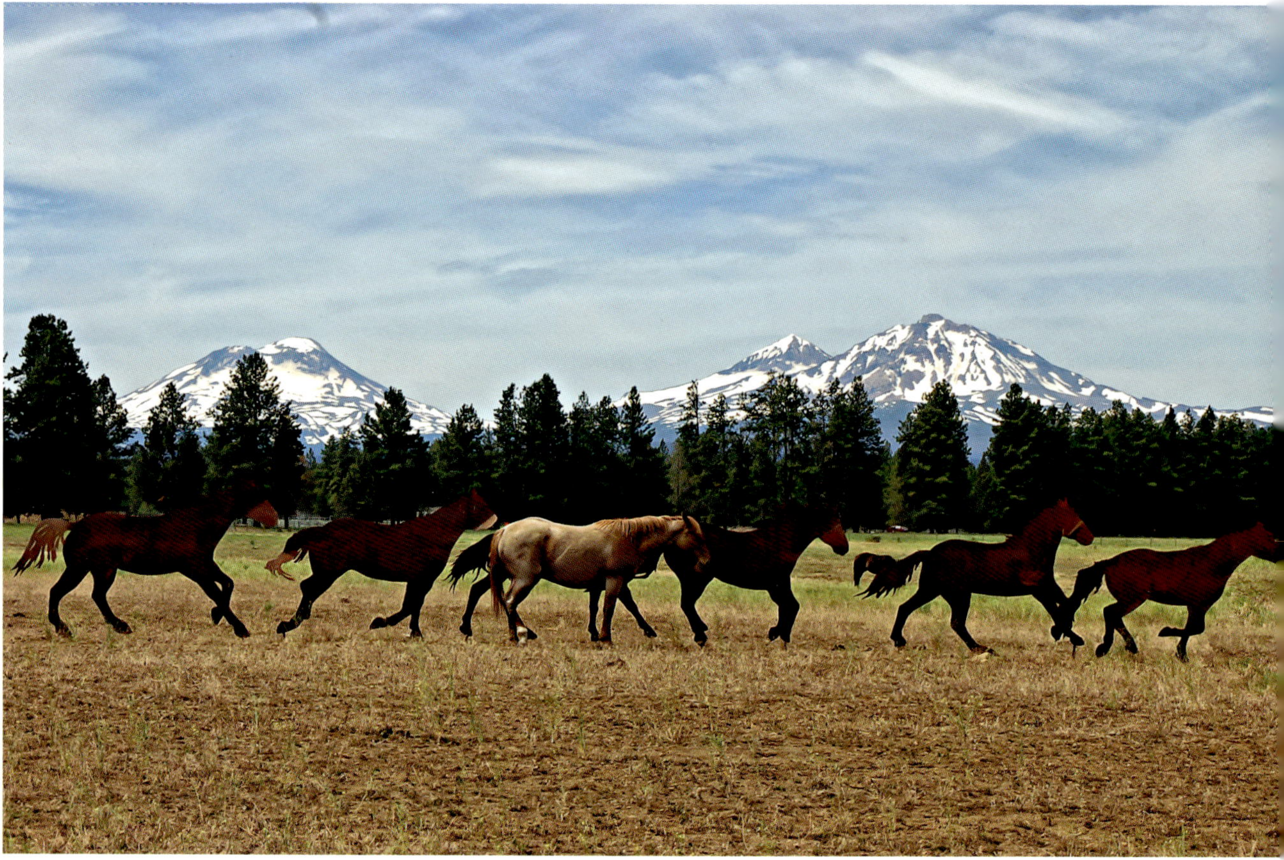

Lone horse on Highway 20. The Three Sister Mountains are the backdrop for these metal horse sculptures created by Brian Bain, commissioned by Sisters to commemorate the town's ranching and equestrian heritage. *Photo by Barbara Tricarico.*

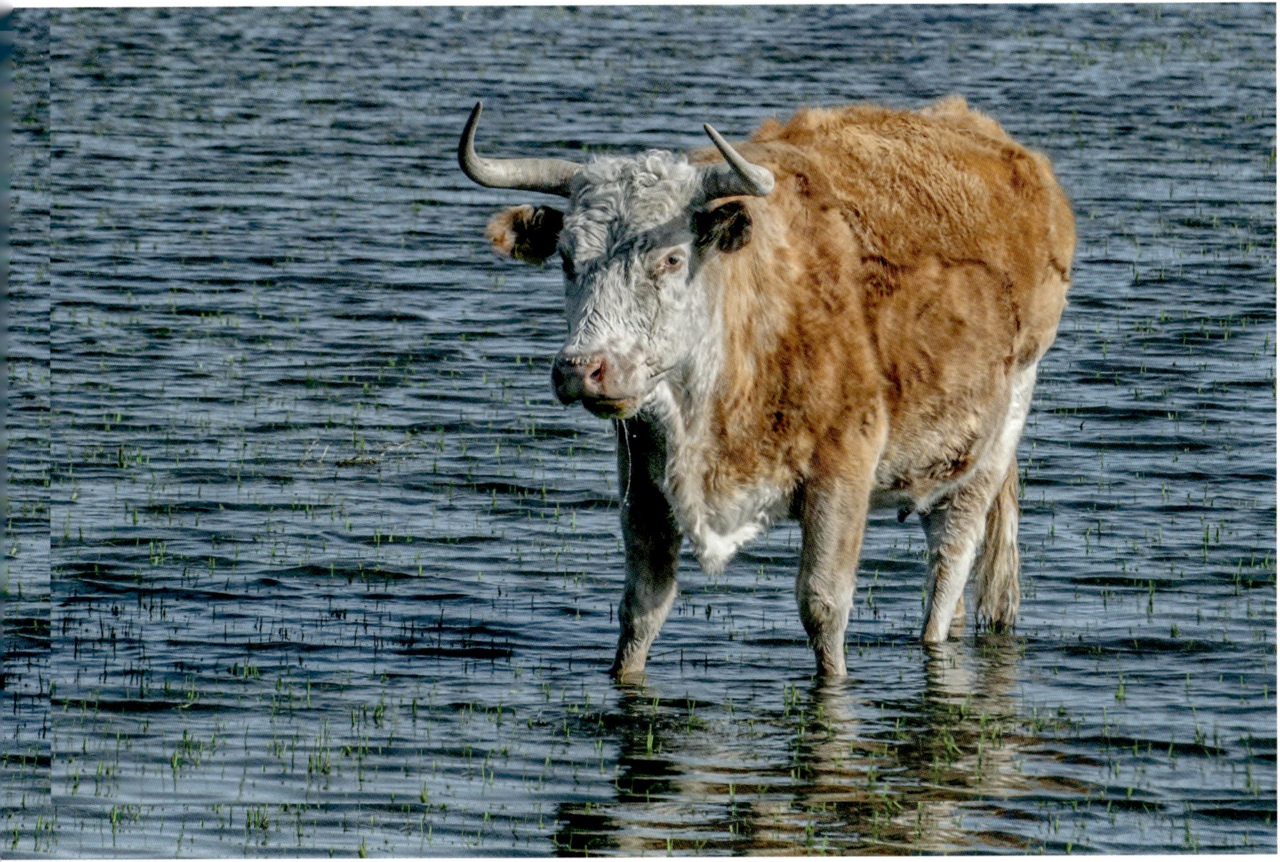

Thirsty steer. *Photo by George F. Peterson.*

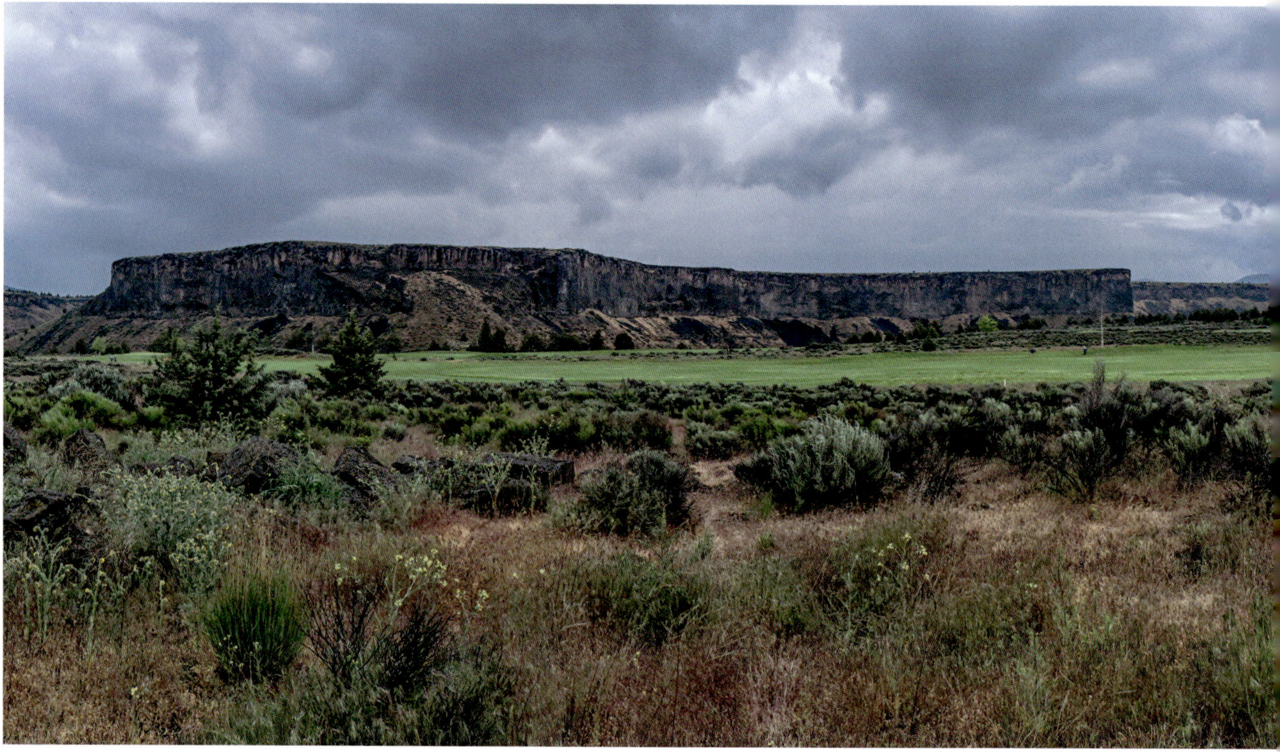

Crooked River Canyon. The Crooked River sits beneath these 400-foot cliffs. The Crooked River Ranch and Golf Course is adjacent to the river. *Photo by Barbara Tricarico.*

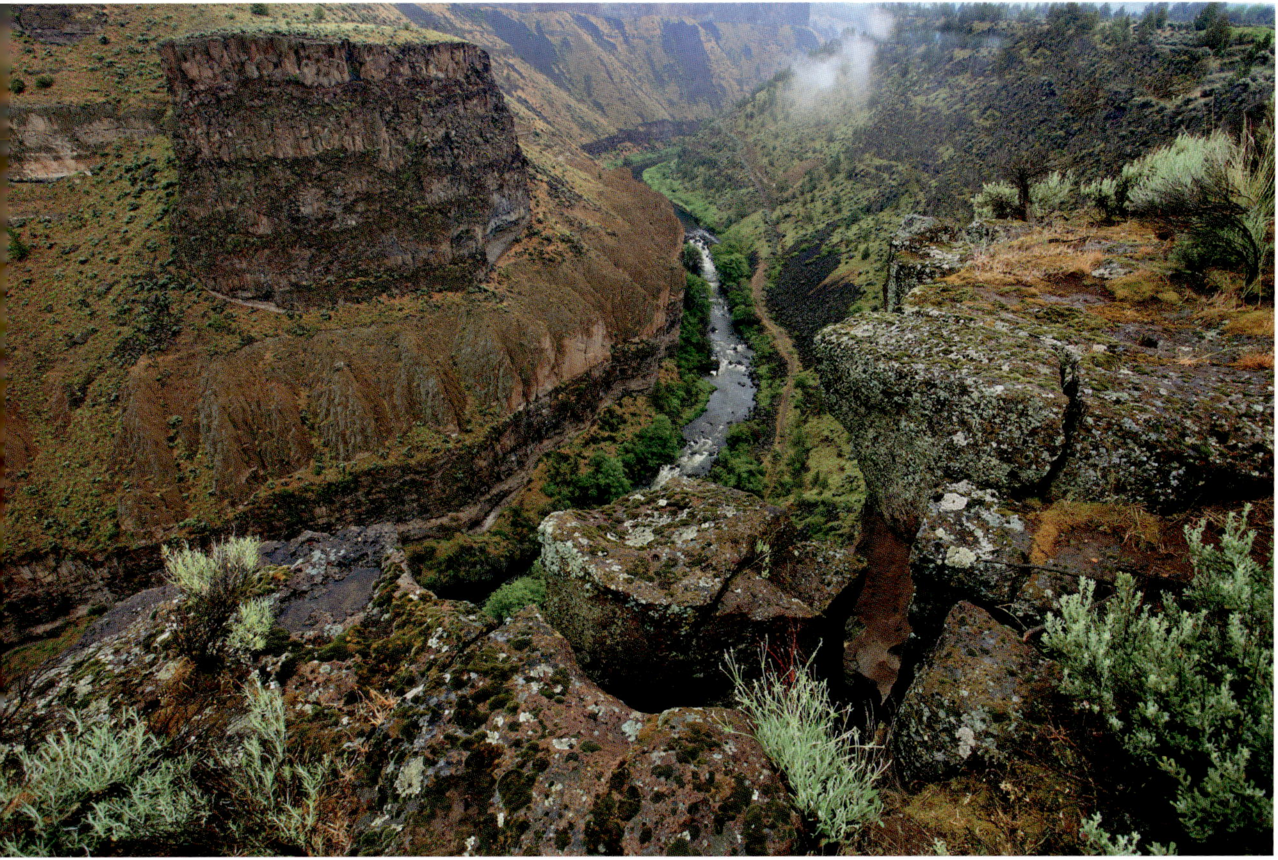

Deschutes River Canyon. *Photo by Neal R. Thompson.*

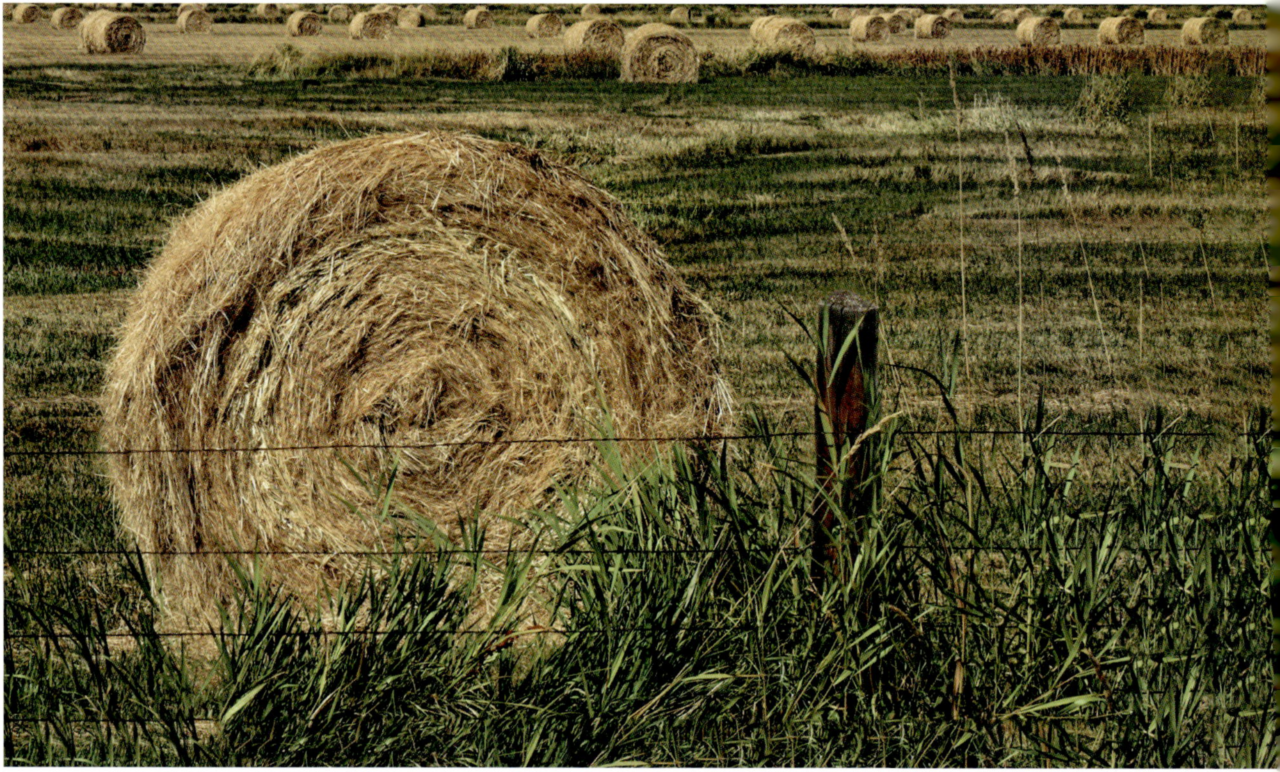

 Bales of hay. *Photo by Andrea Shapiro.*

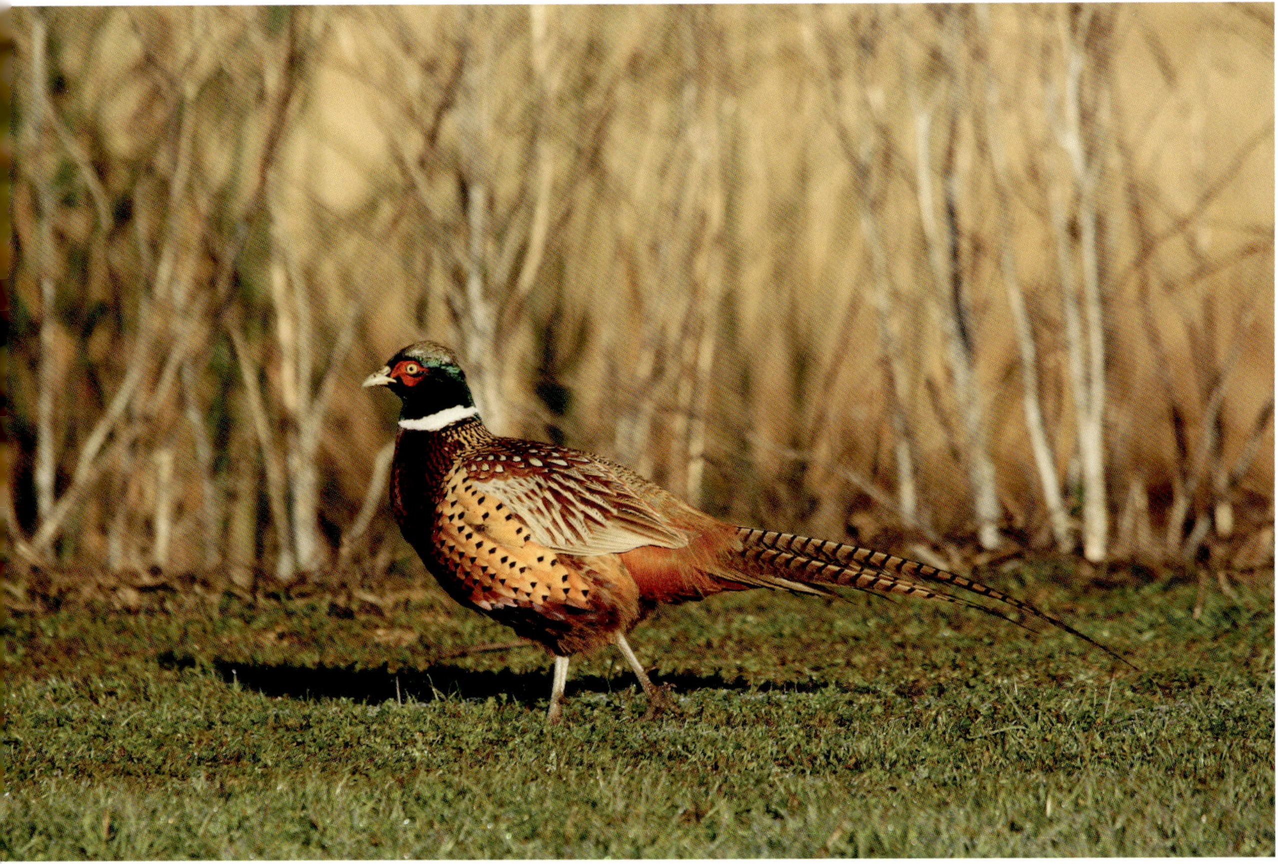

Pheasant. *Photo by Dan Elster.*

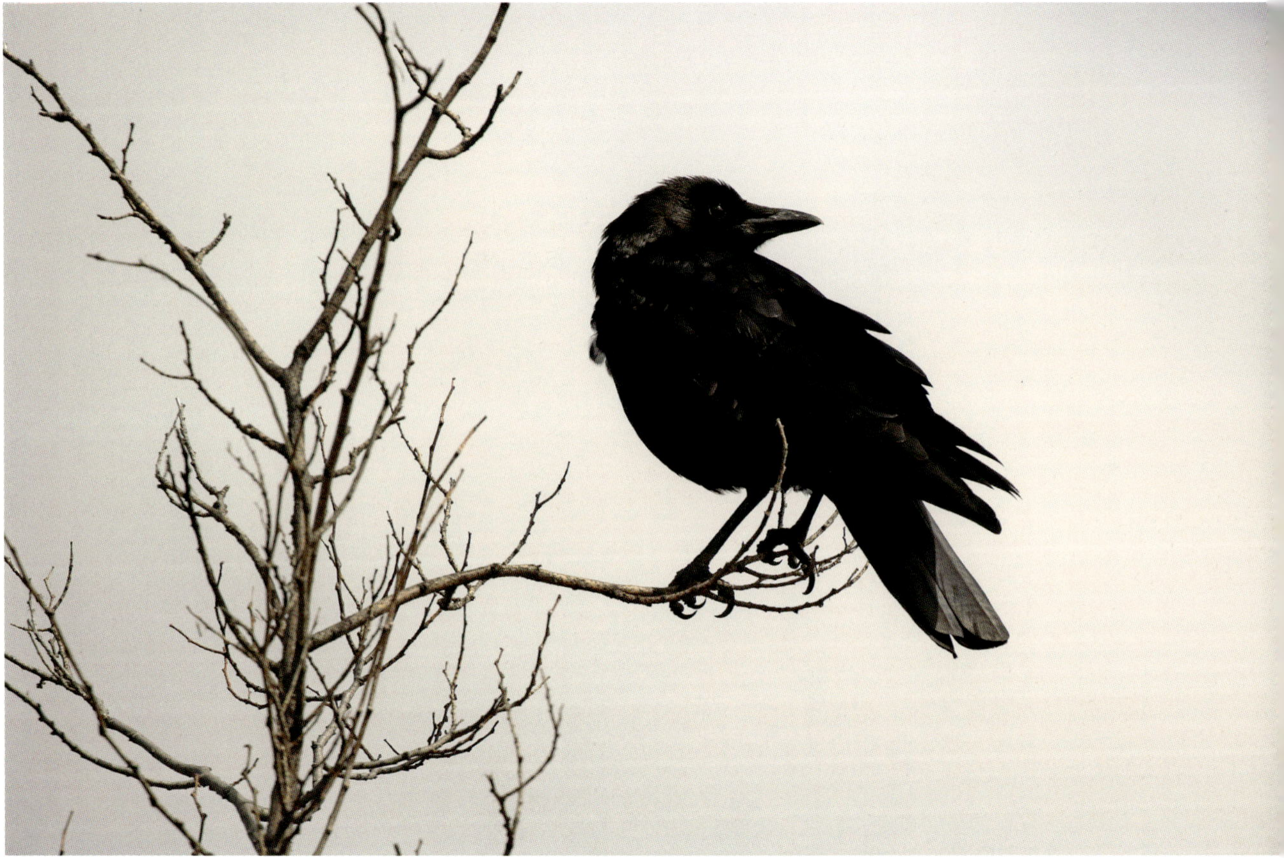

 Crow. *Photo by Dan Elster.*

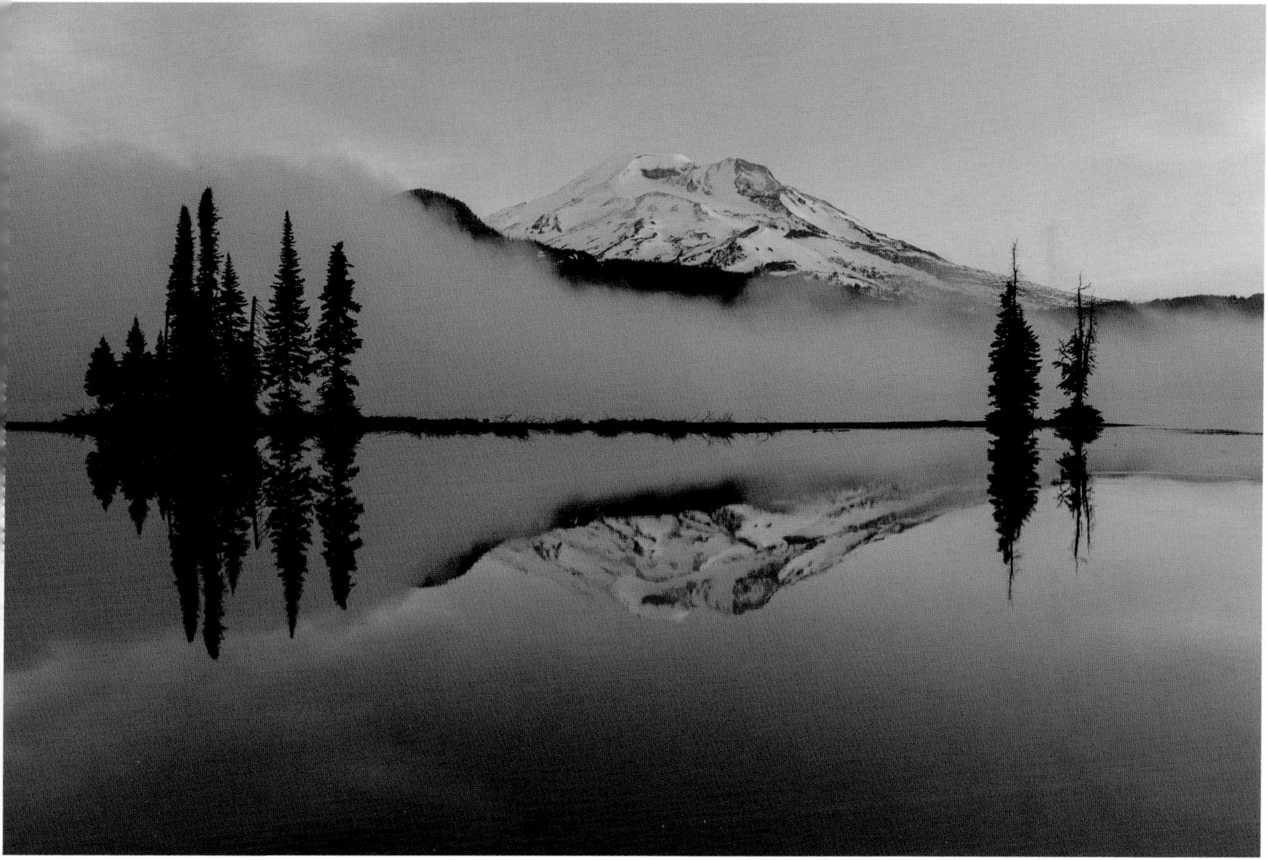

South Sister Mountain from Sparks Lake. *Photo by Vldn Taylor.*

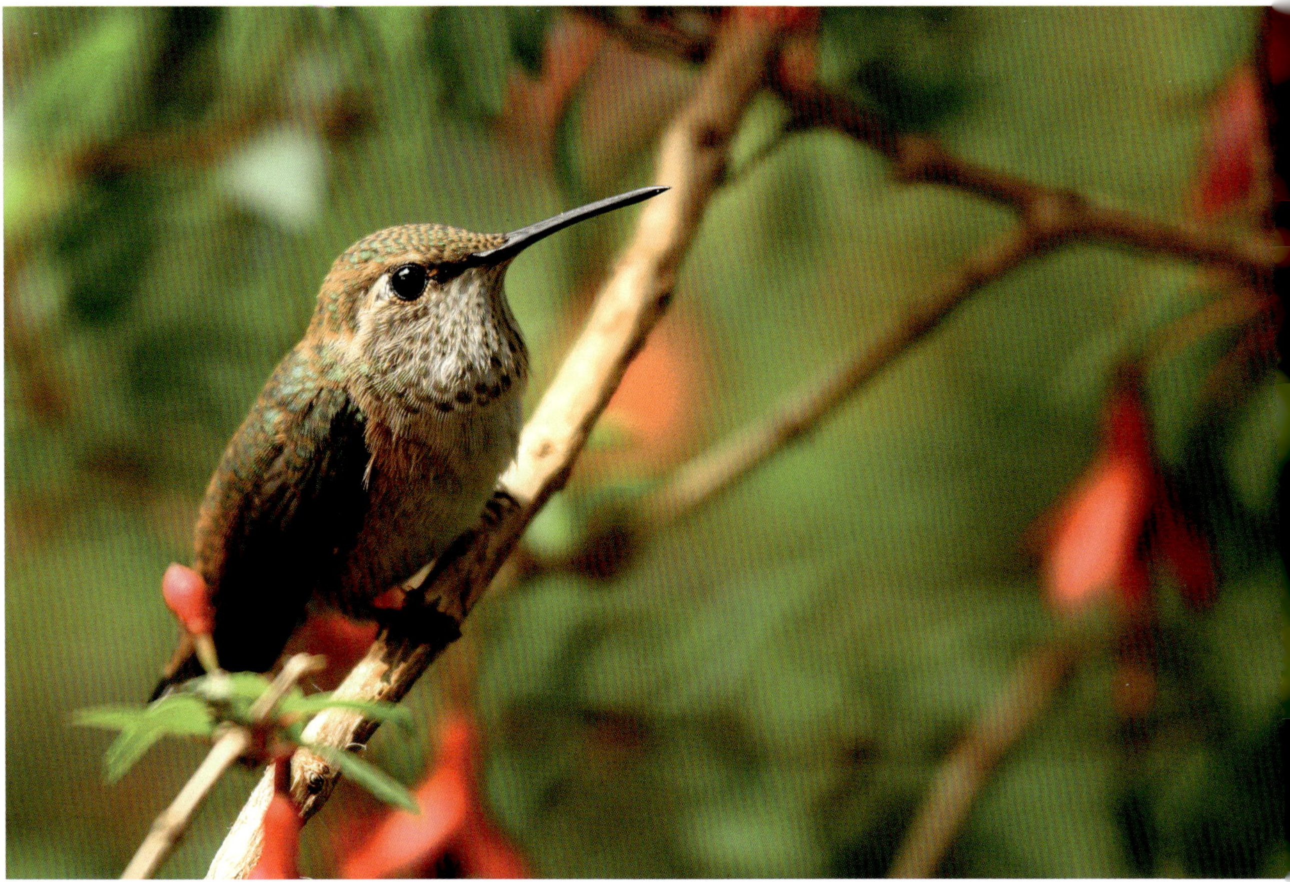

 Rufous hummingbird. *Photo by Dan Elster.*

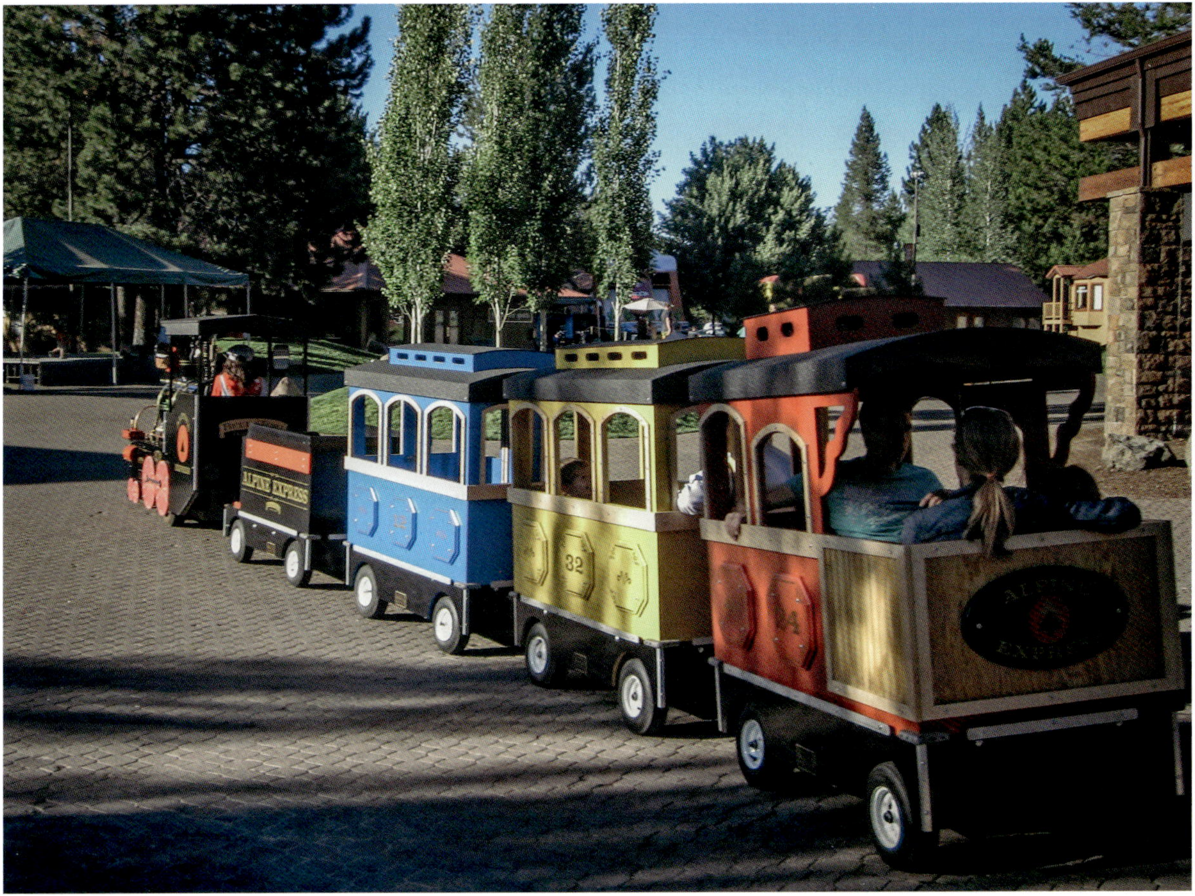

Sunriver Village train. *Photo by Diana Standing.*

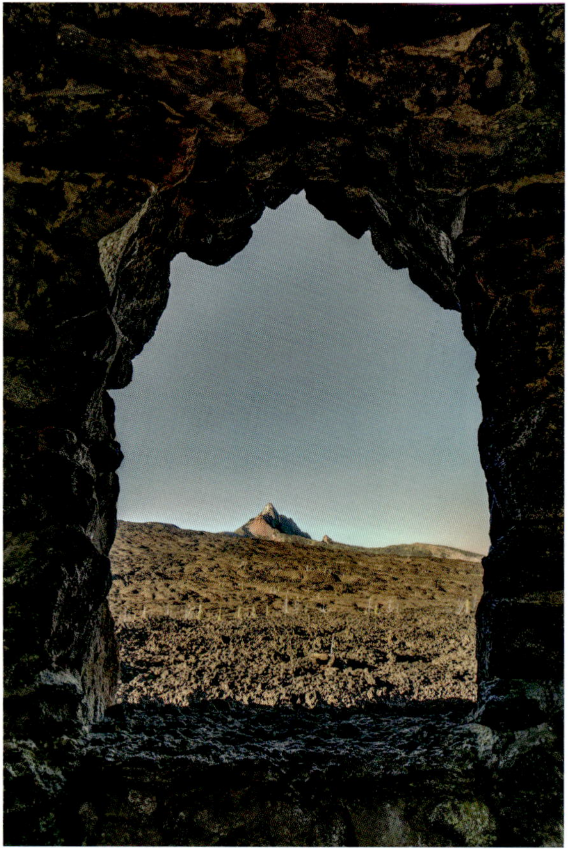

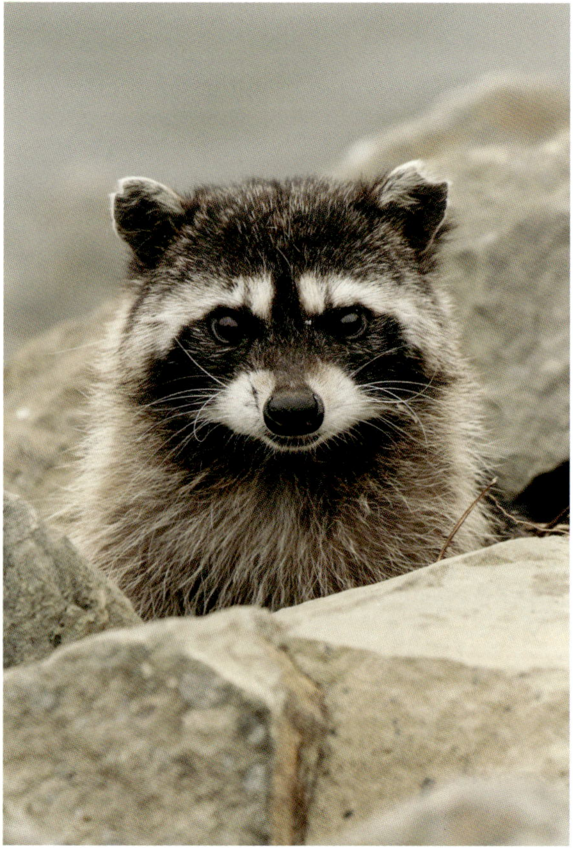

Mount Washington as seen from lava fields surrounding Dee Wright Observatory, at the summit of McKenzie Pass. The pass has an elevation of 5,325 feet and is open only about four months of the year due to snow. *Photo by Sue Newman.* • Raccoon. *Photo by Dan Elster.*

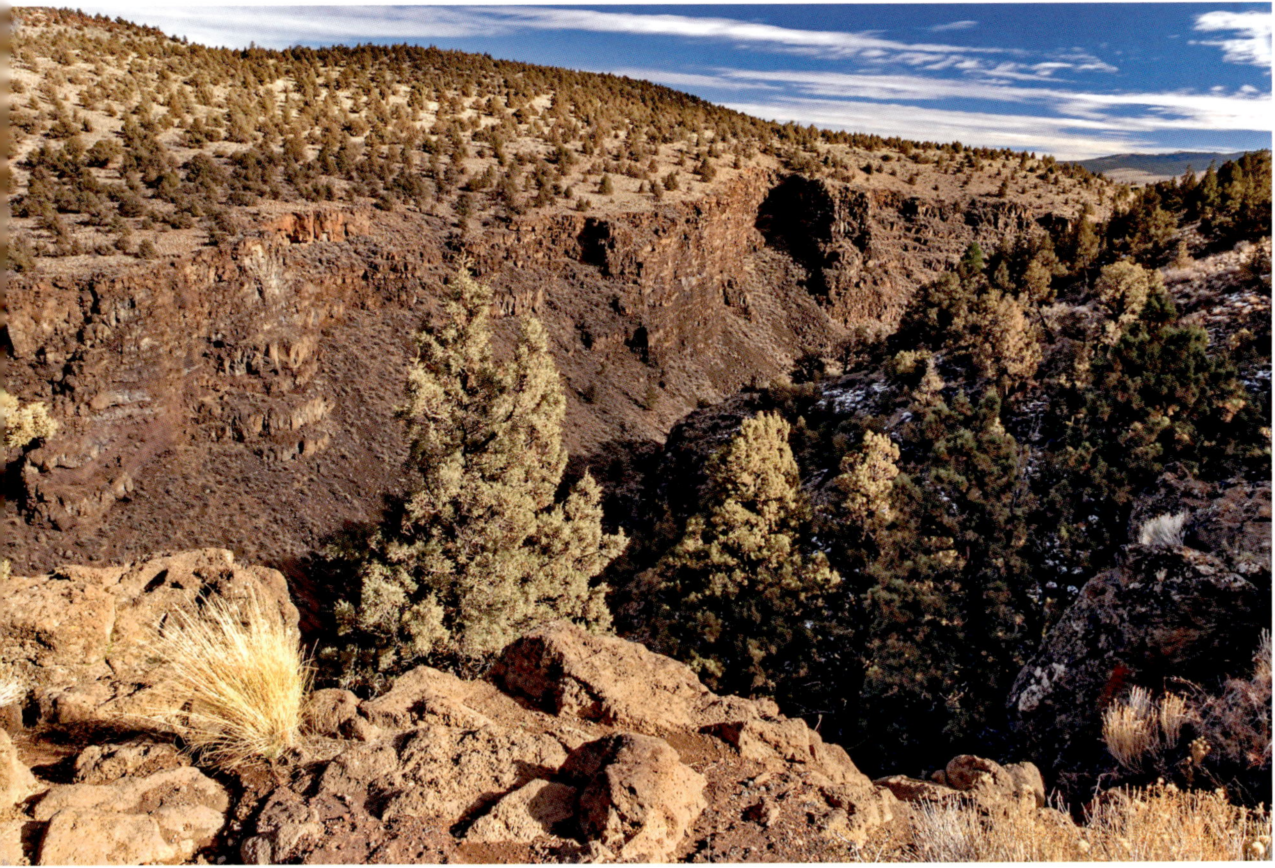

Dry River Canyon off Highway 20, near Bend. *Photo by Jay Newman.*

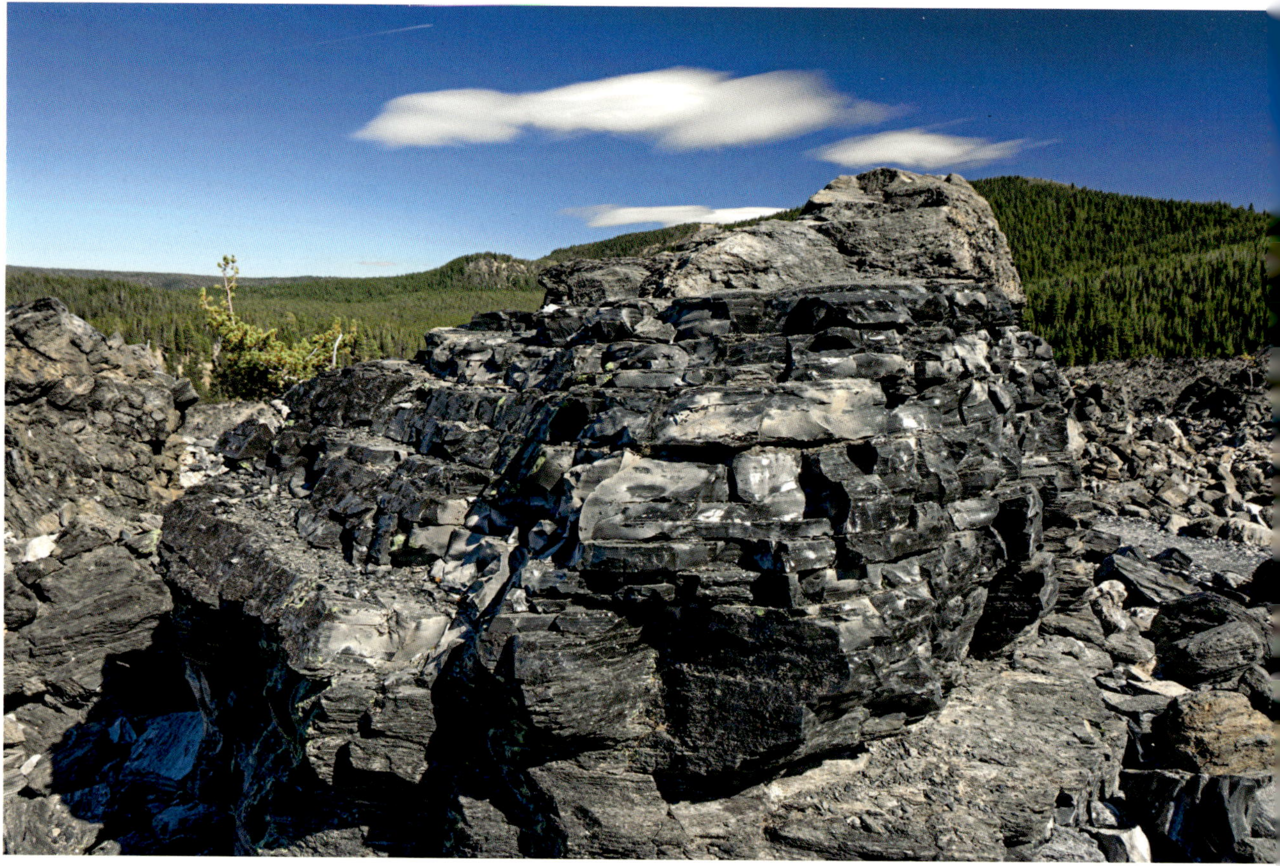

 Big Obsidian Flow. This glassy black obsidian and gray pumice lava was formed 1,300 years ago near Newberry Caldera. *Photo by Jay Newm*

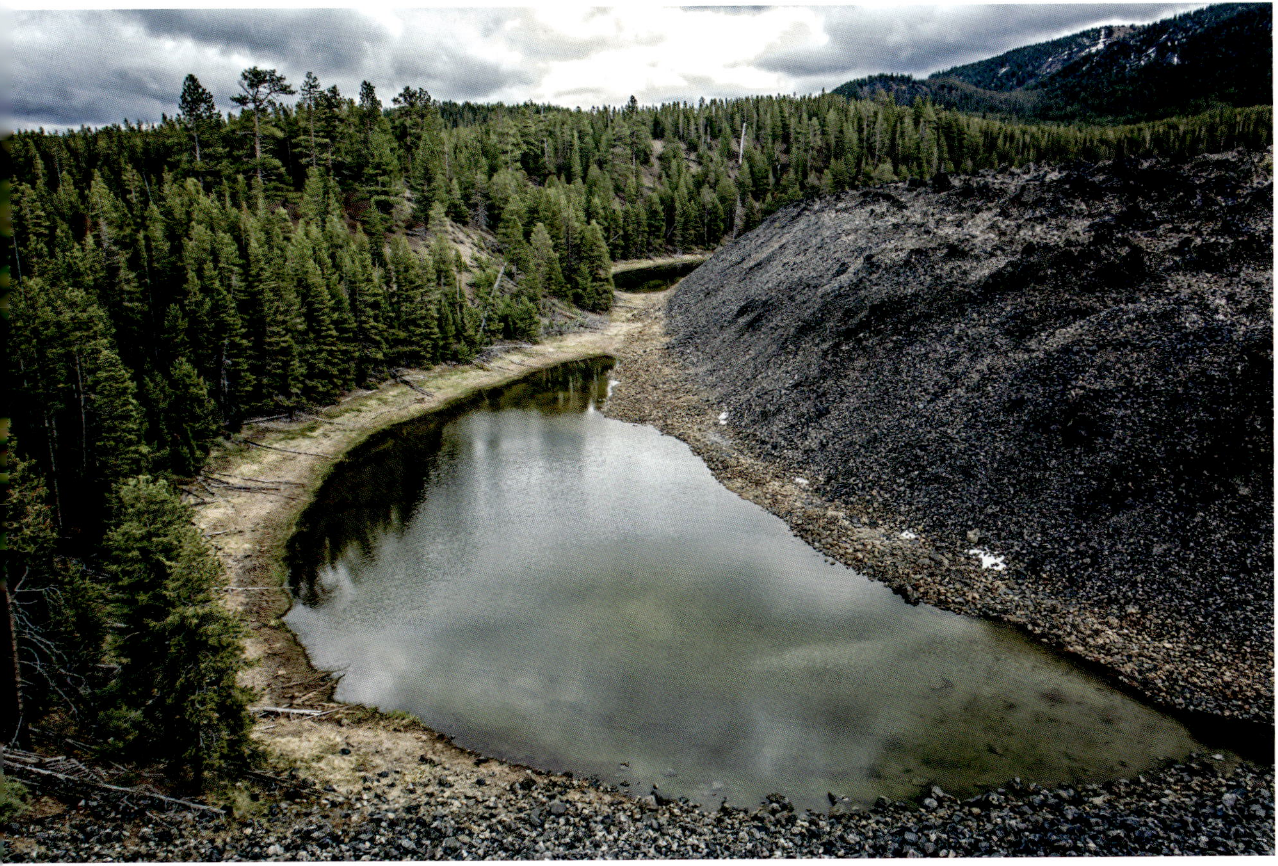

Lost Lake, at the edge of the Big Obsidian Flow Interpretive Trail. This lava flow is the youngest in Oregon and covers about one square mile near Newberry Caldera. *Photo by Barbara Tricarico.*

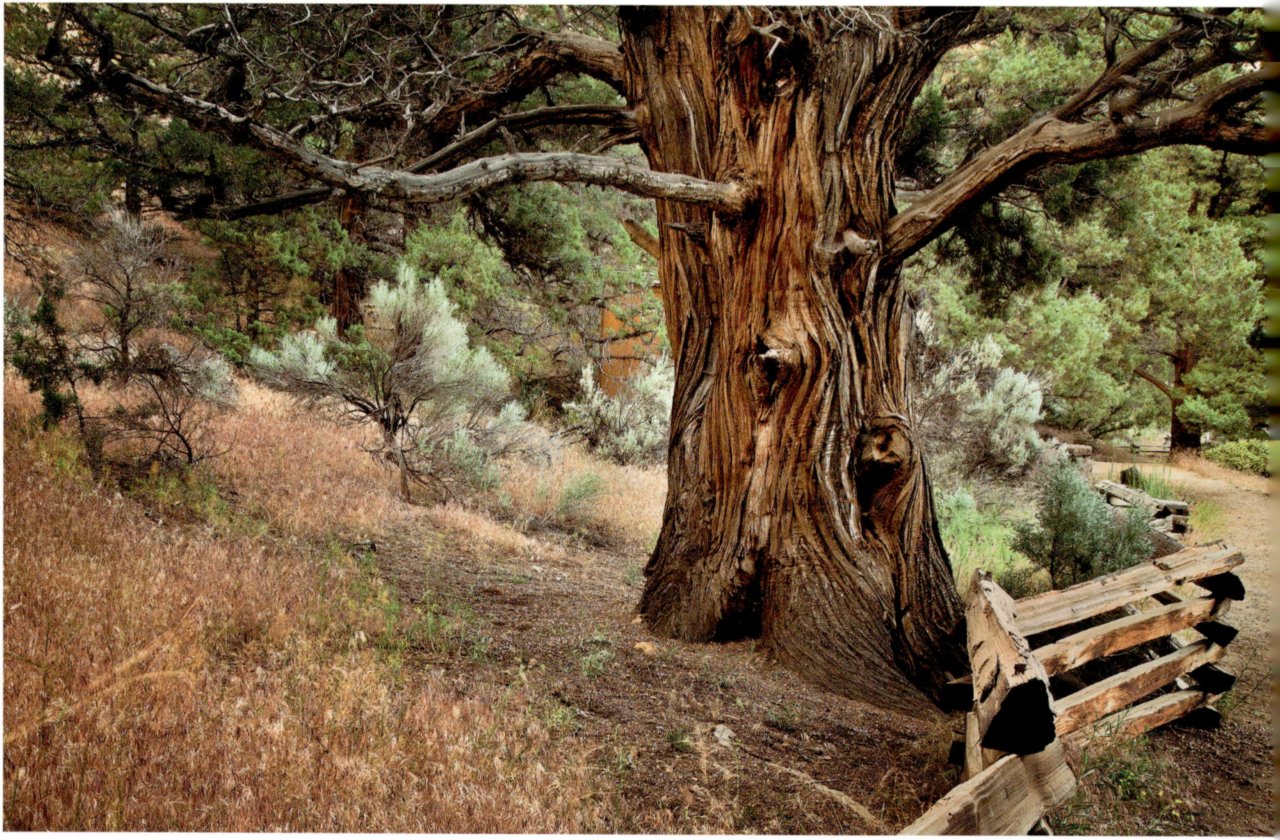

 Old, crooked oak tree near Smith Rock State Park. *Photo by John Christer Petersen.*

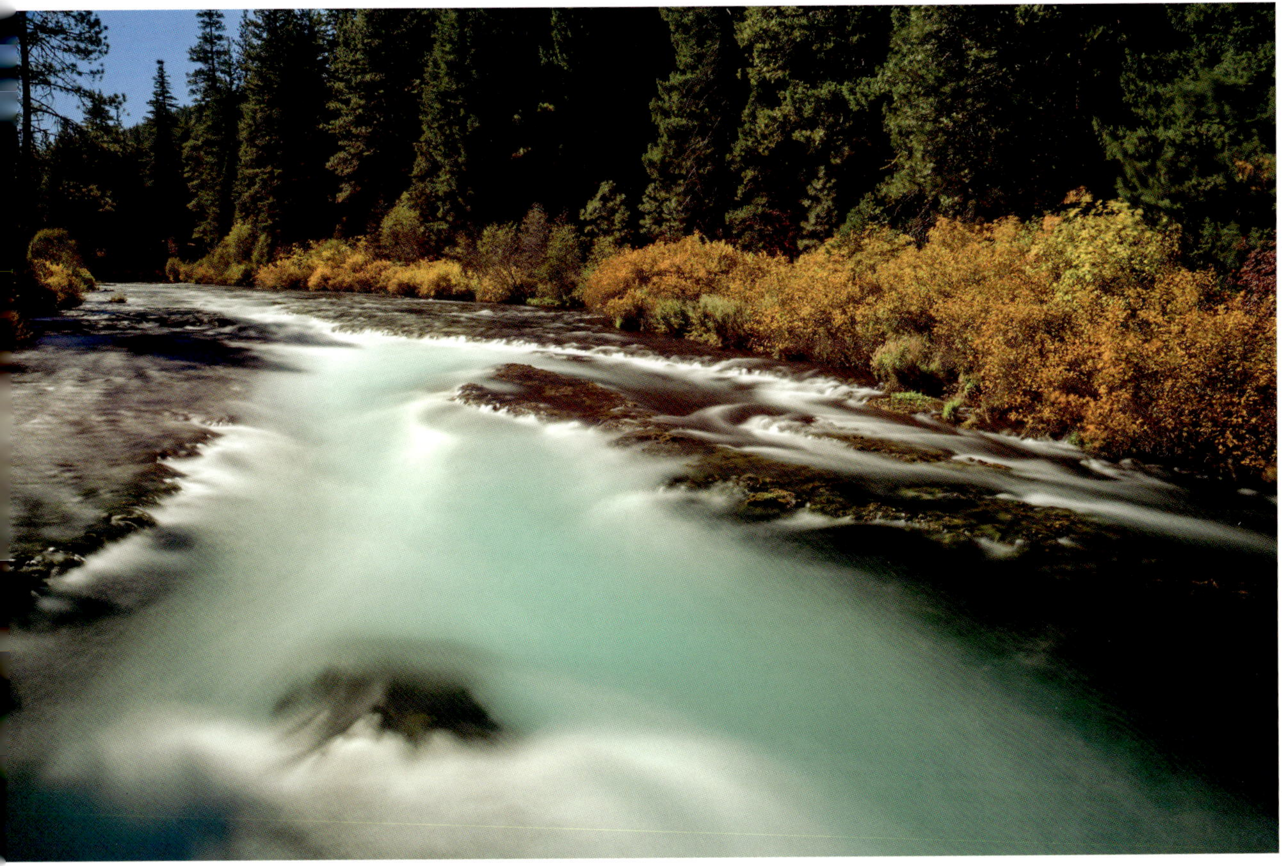

The Metolius River, a tributary of the Deschutes River near Sisters, is popular for fly-fishing. *Photo by Jay Newman.*

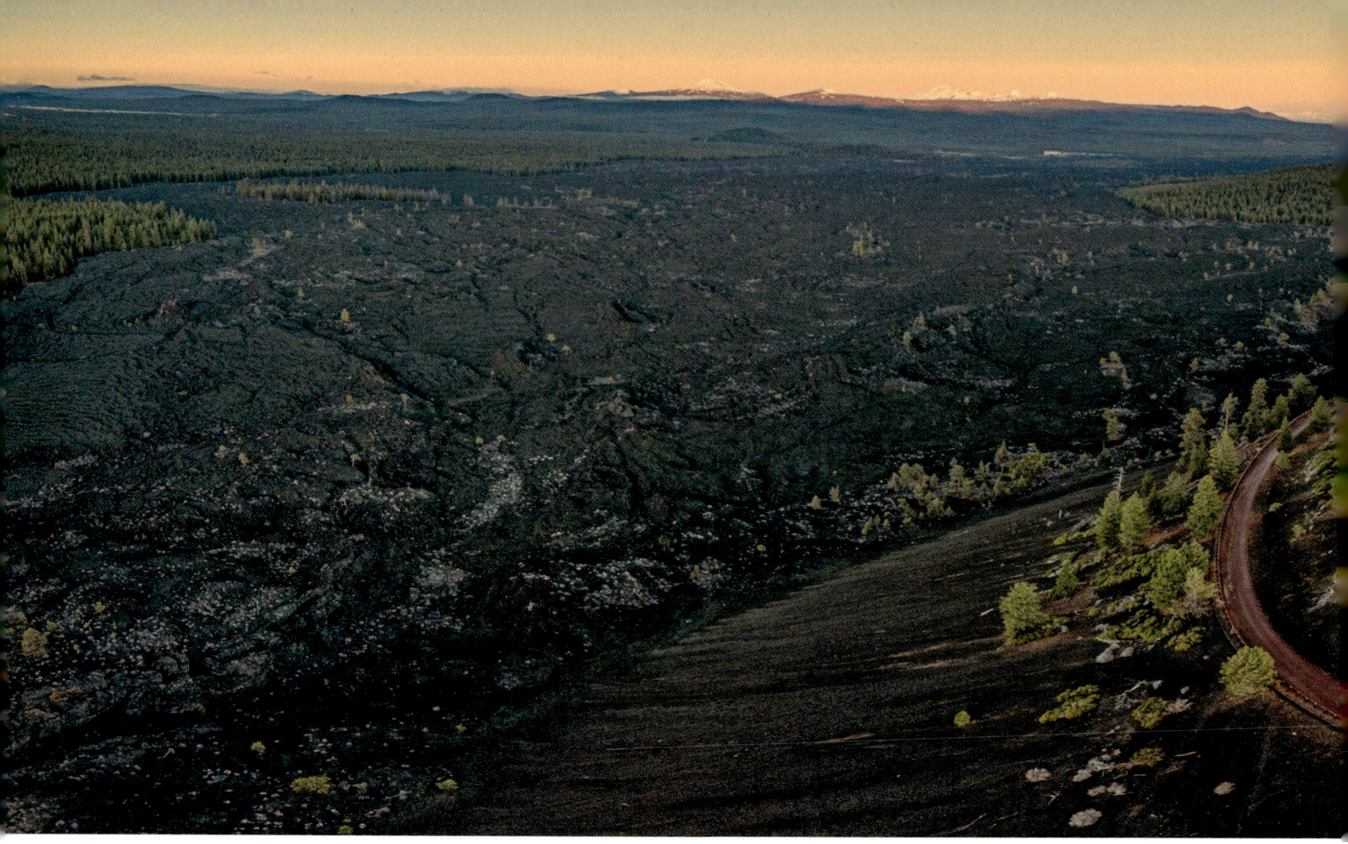

Lava Butte. Near Sunriver and Bend, Lava Butte is a cinder cone and part of the Newberry National Volcanic Monument. It was caused by a single eruption about 7,000 years ago. At the top of the spiral road is a US Forest Service lookout tower built in 1931. In 1966, astronauts trained here for the moon landings. *Photo by Mason Marsh.*

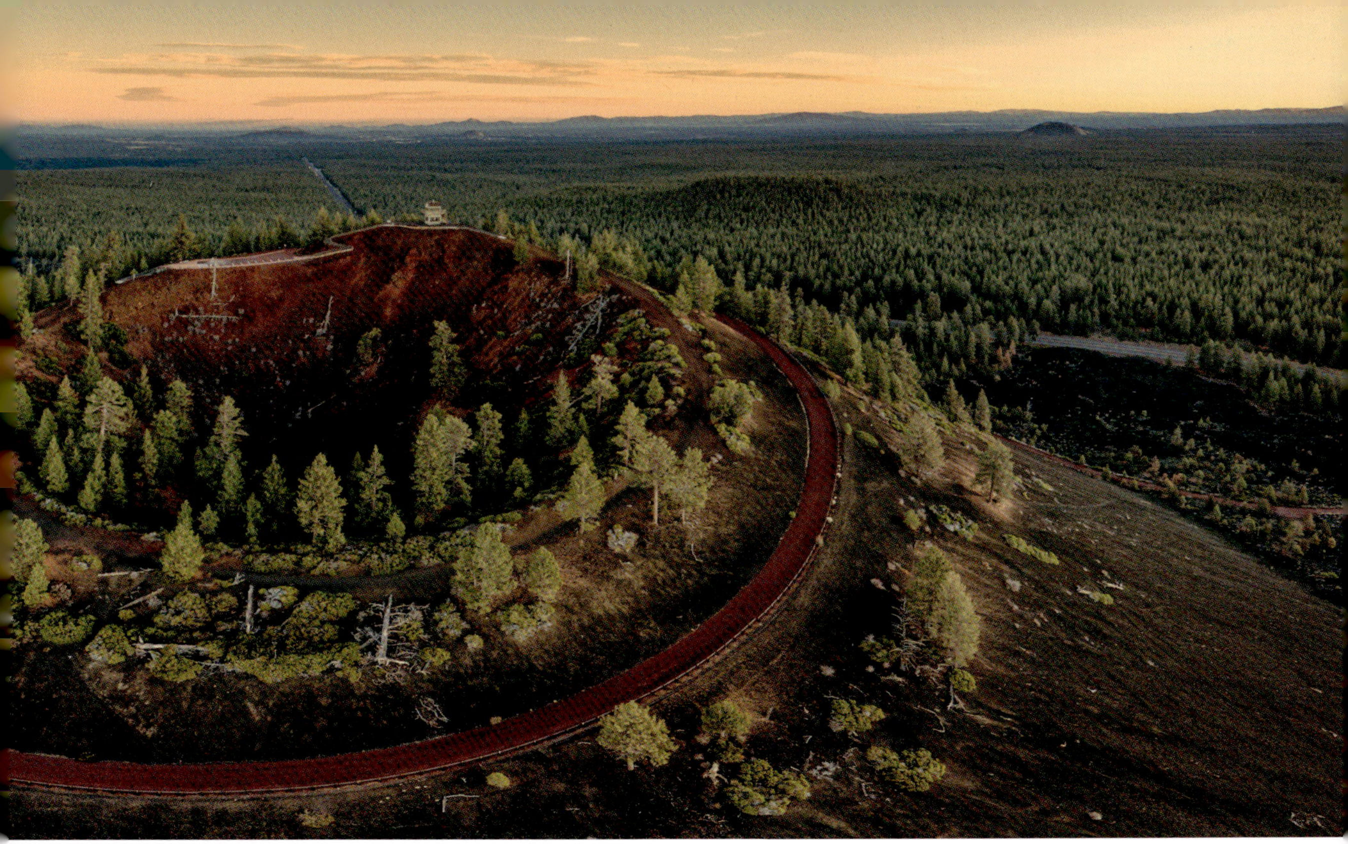

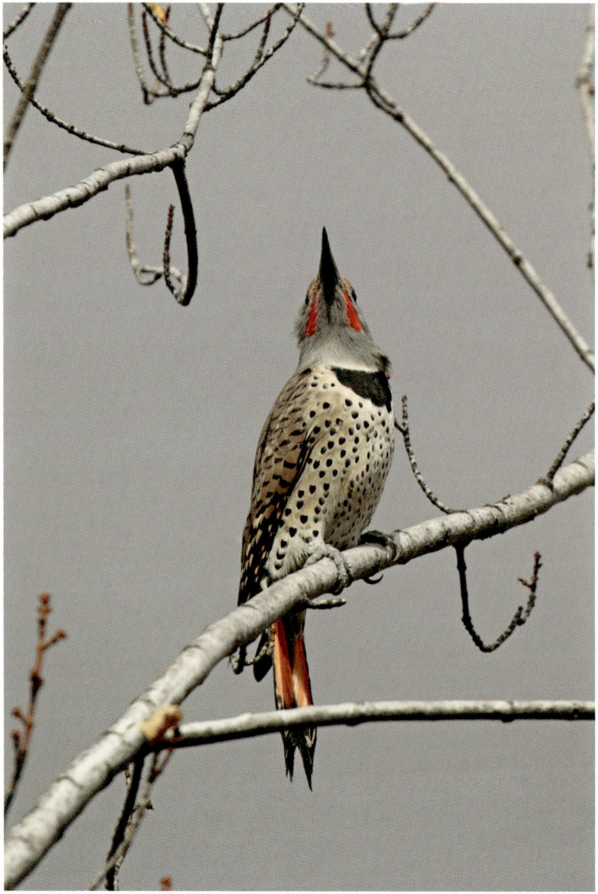

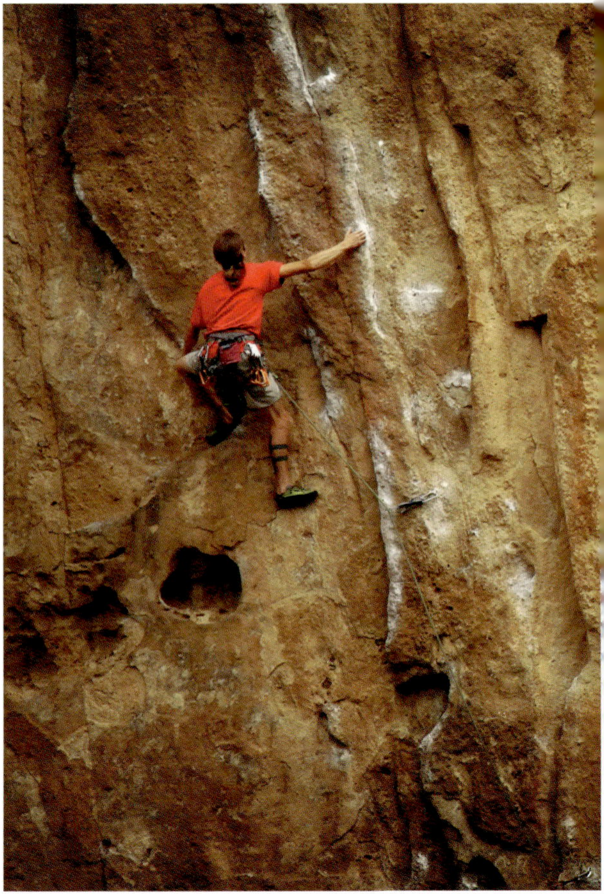

 Flicker. *Photo by Dan Elster.* • Rock climber, Smith Rock State Park. *Photo by John Kirk.*

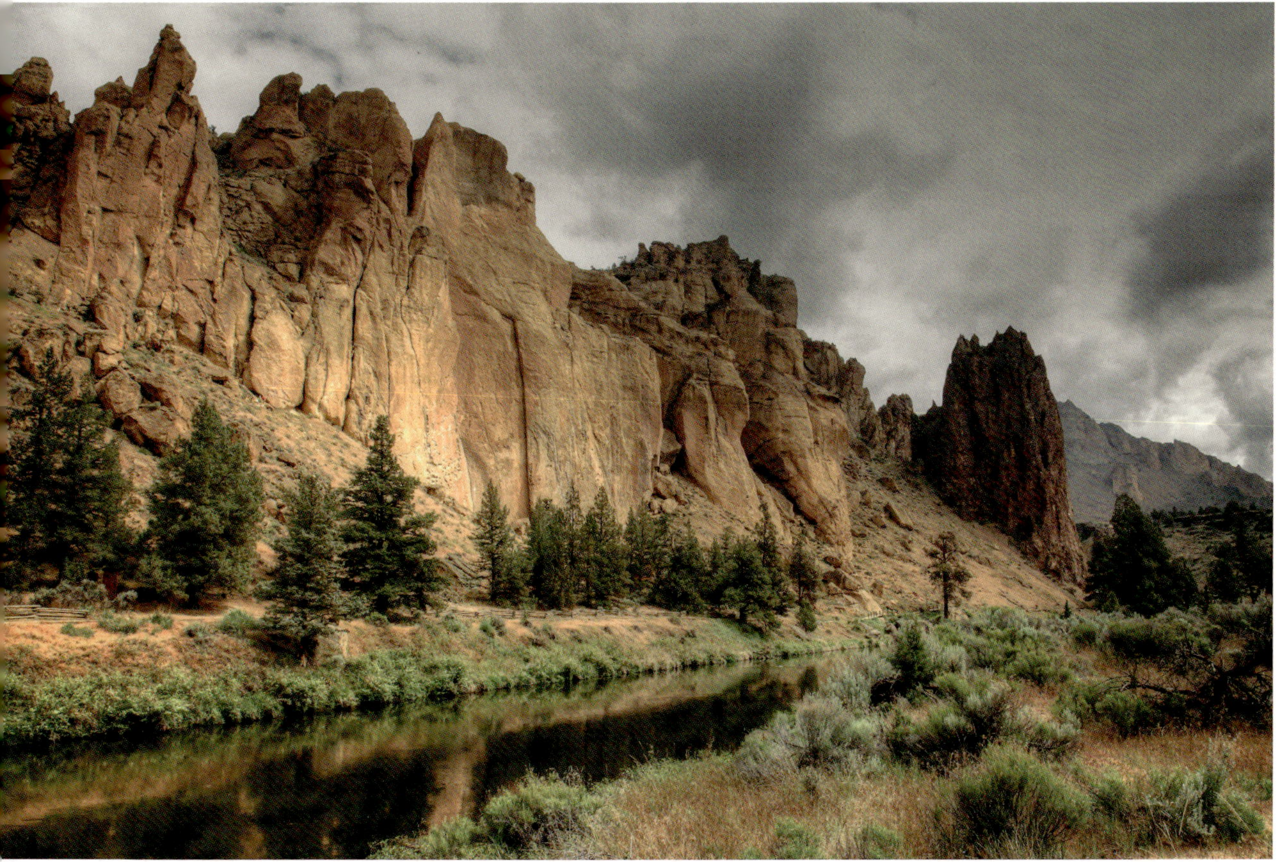

Smith Rock. *Photo by John Kirk.*

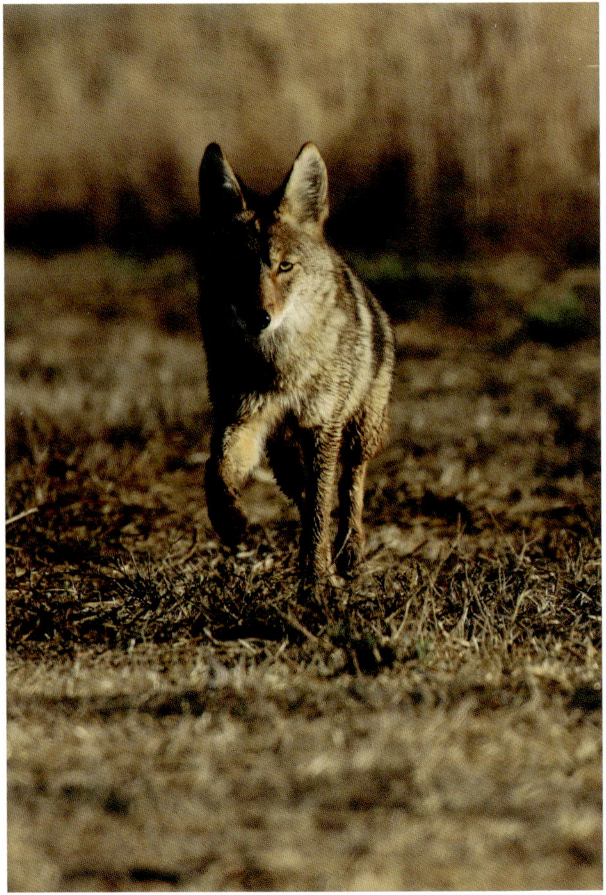

 Coyote. *Photo by Dan Elster.*

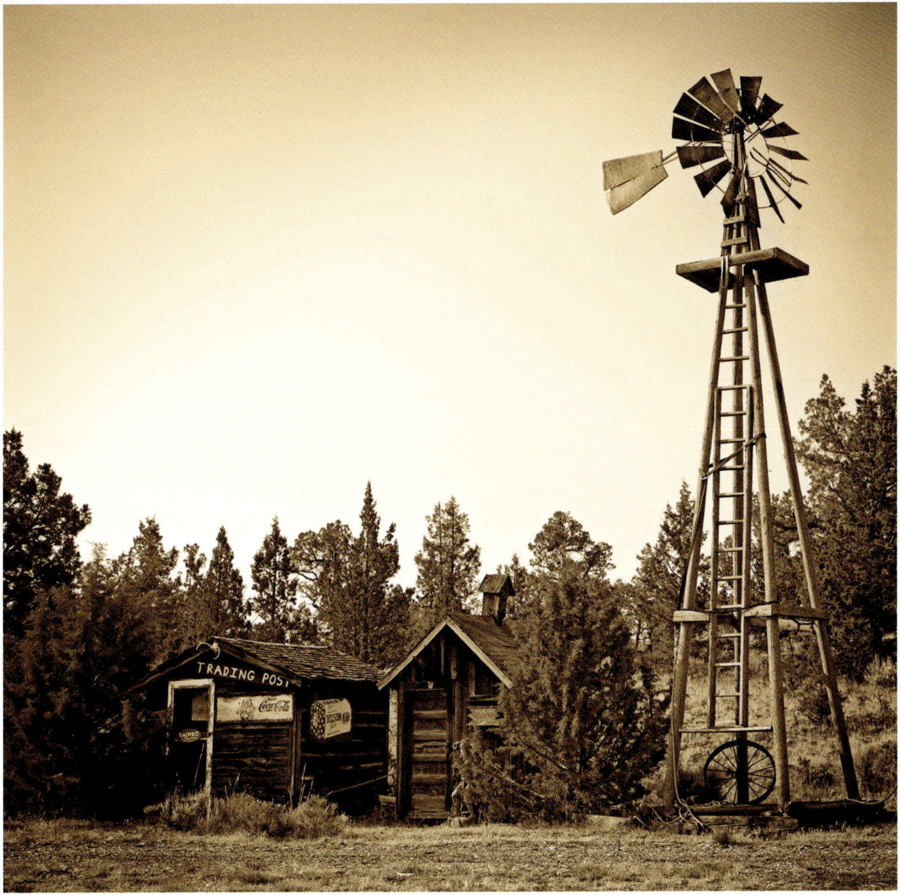

Sisters Old Trading Post. *Photo by John Christer Petersen.*

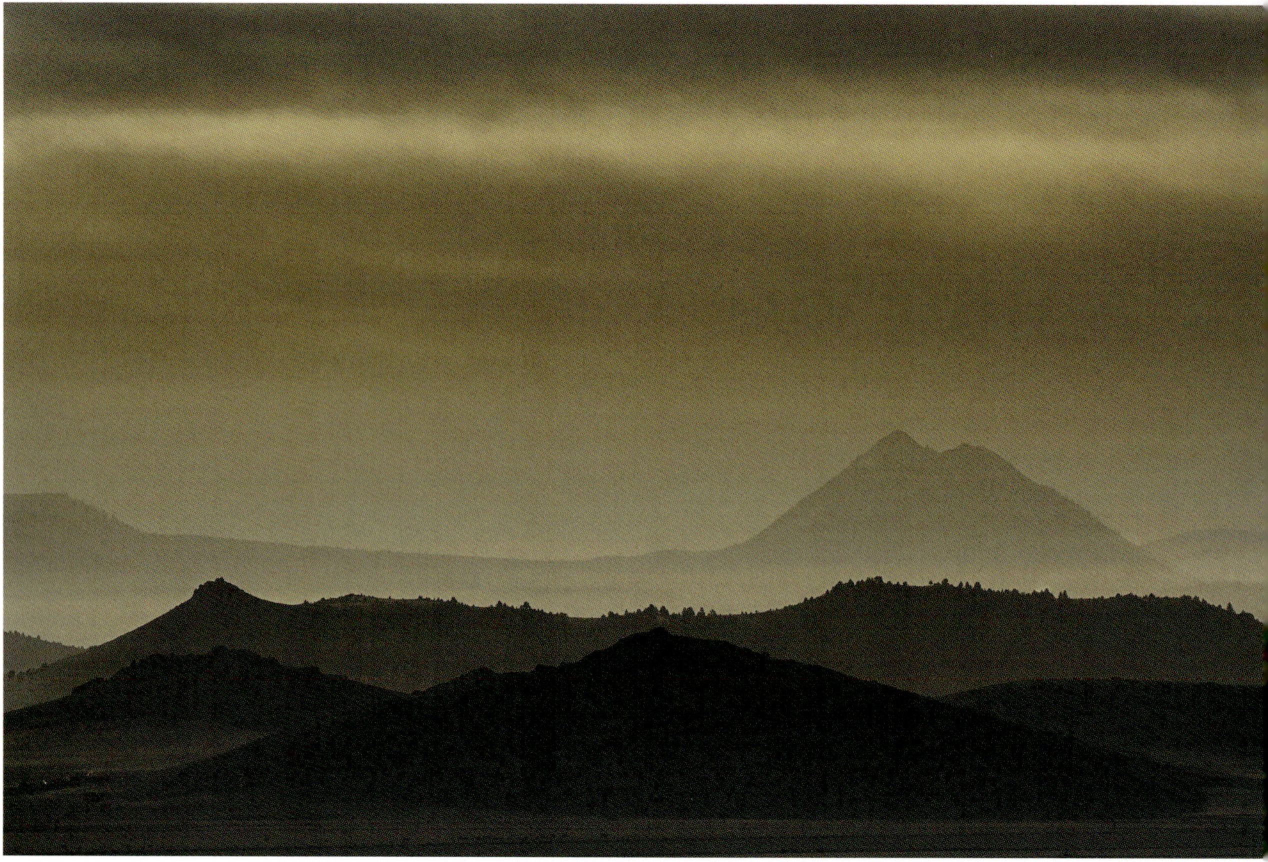

 Black Butte landscape. Black Butte is an extinct volcano and a popular hiking location. *Photo by David Lorenz Winston.*

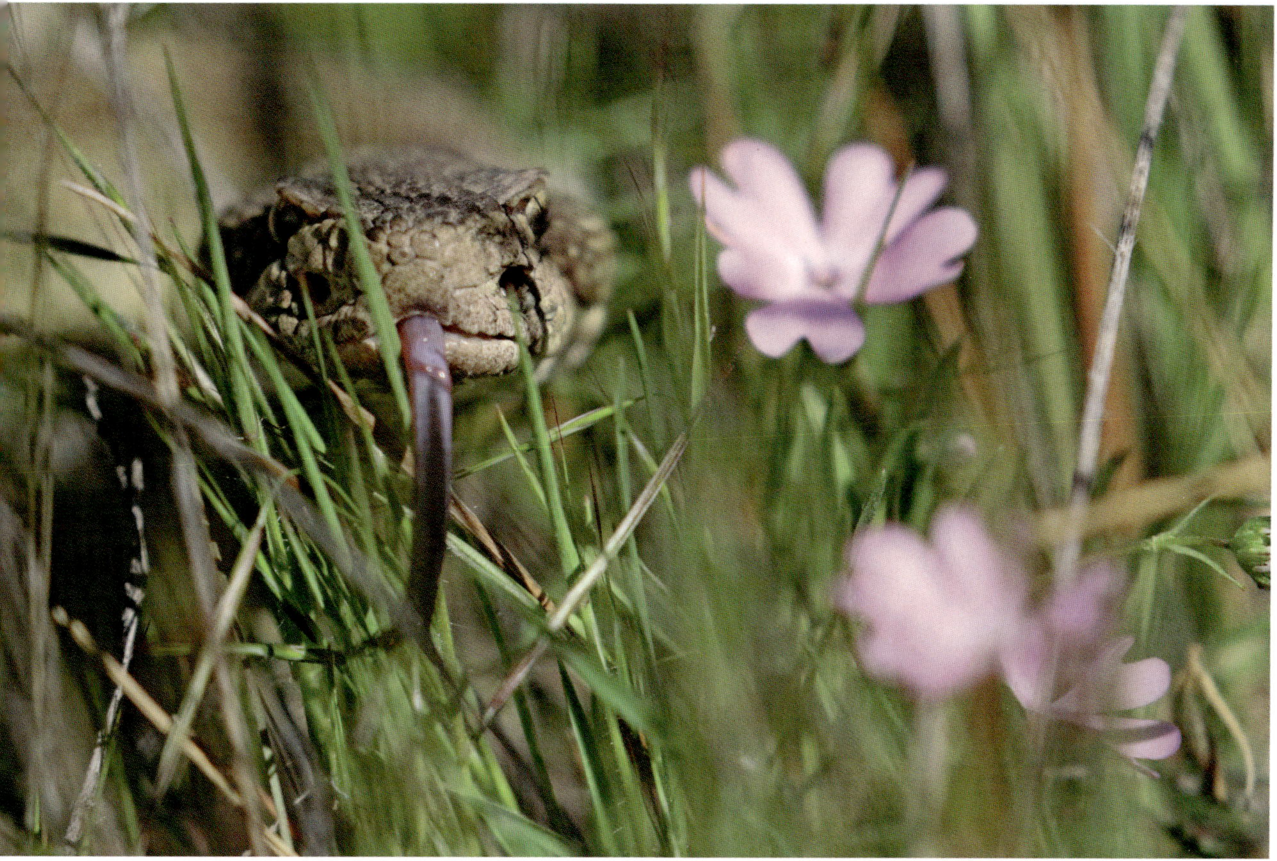

Northern Pacific rattlesnake. *Photo by Dan Elster.*

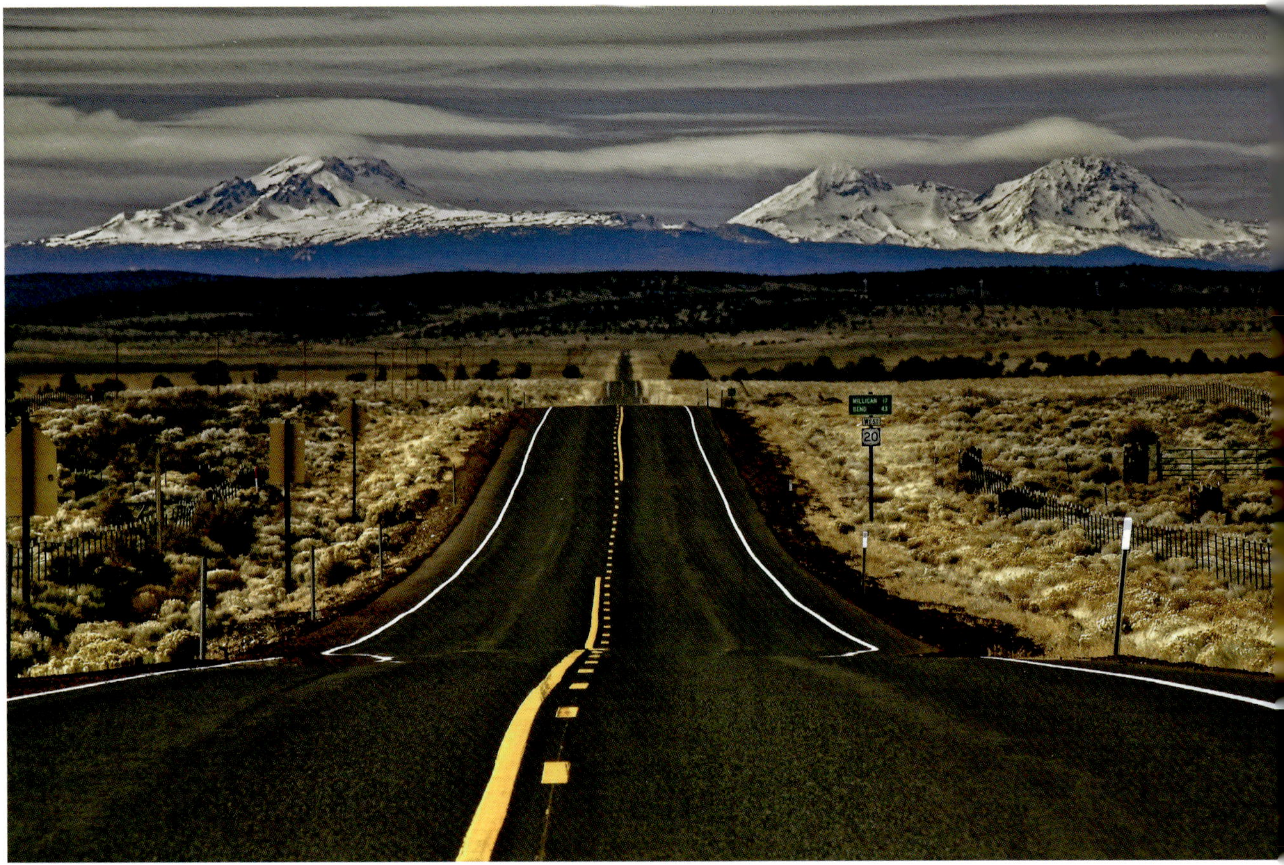

 Highway 20, with views of Middle Sister, North Sister, and Broken Top Mountains. *Photo by Jay Newman.*

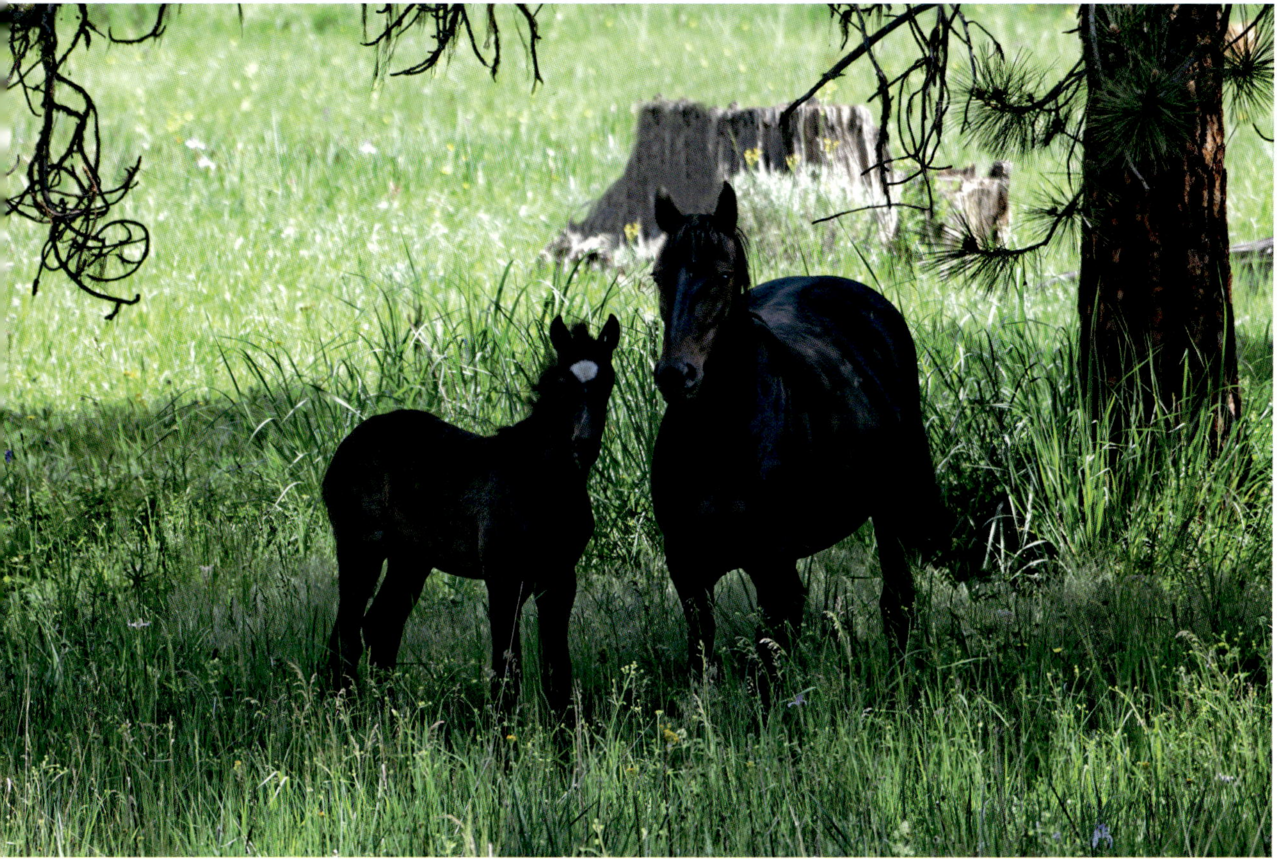

Wild foal and mare at Ochoco National Forest. *Photo by Barbara Tricarico.*

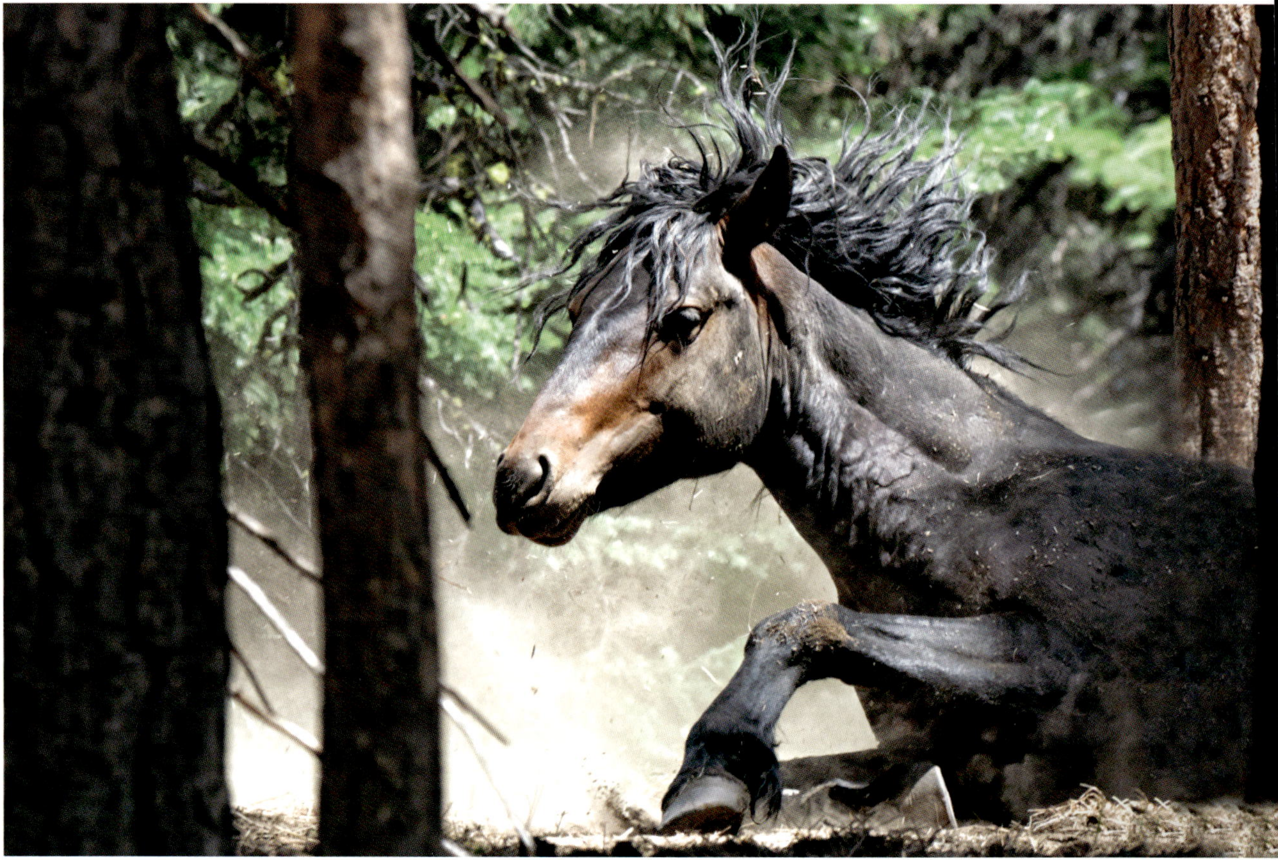

 Bathing in the dust. Wild horse at Ochoco National Forest. *Photo by Barbara Tricarico.*

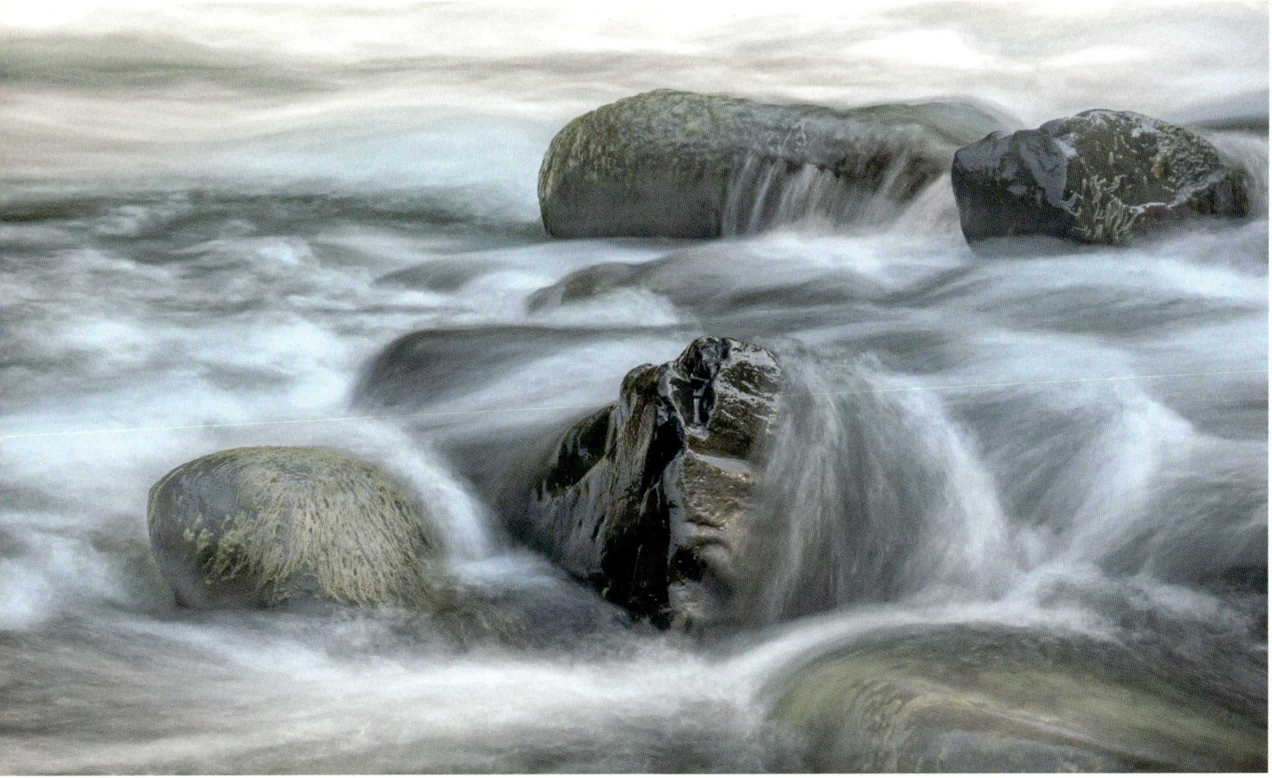

Brietenbush River. *Photo by Vivian McAleavey.*

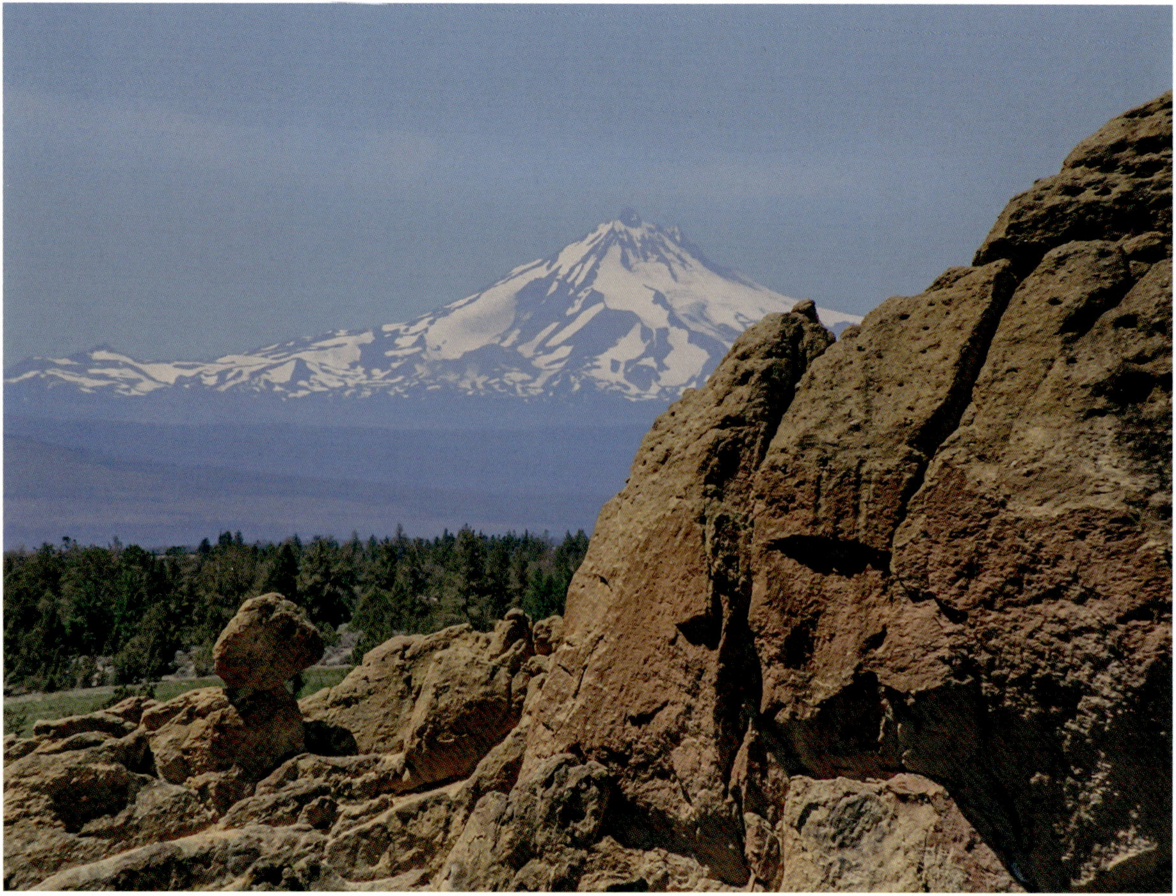

 Mount Jefferson from Smith Rock. Mount Jefferson is the second-tallest mountain in Oregon, after Mount Hood. *Photo by Ken Deveney.*

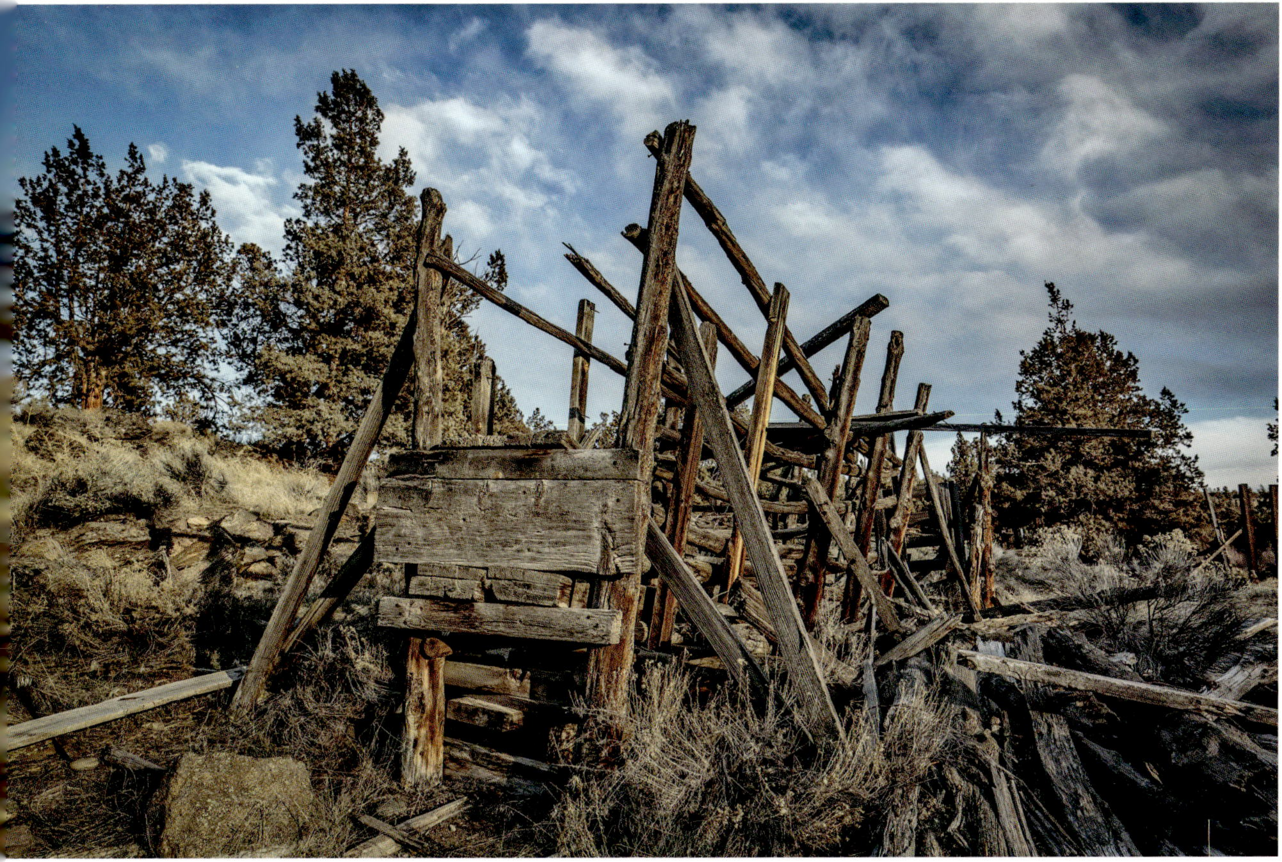

Abandoned cattle-loading ramp near Tumalo. *Photo by Nick Viani.*

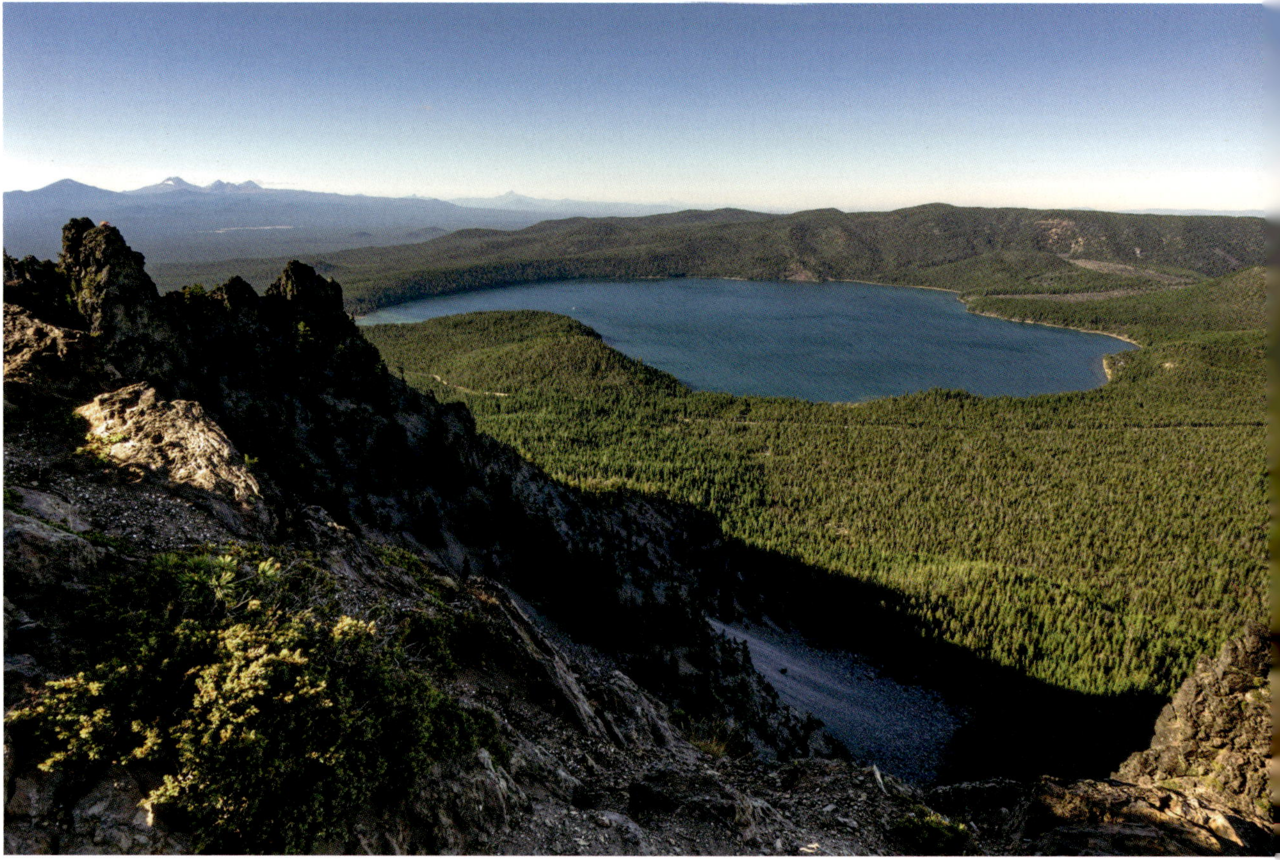

Paulina Lake viewed from Paulina Peak. The lake was formed by 500,000 years of volcanic activity and sits within Newberry Caldera. *Photo by Sue Newman.*

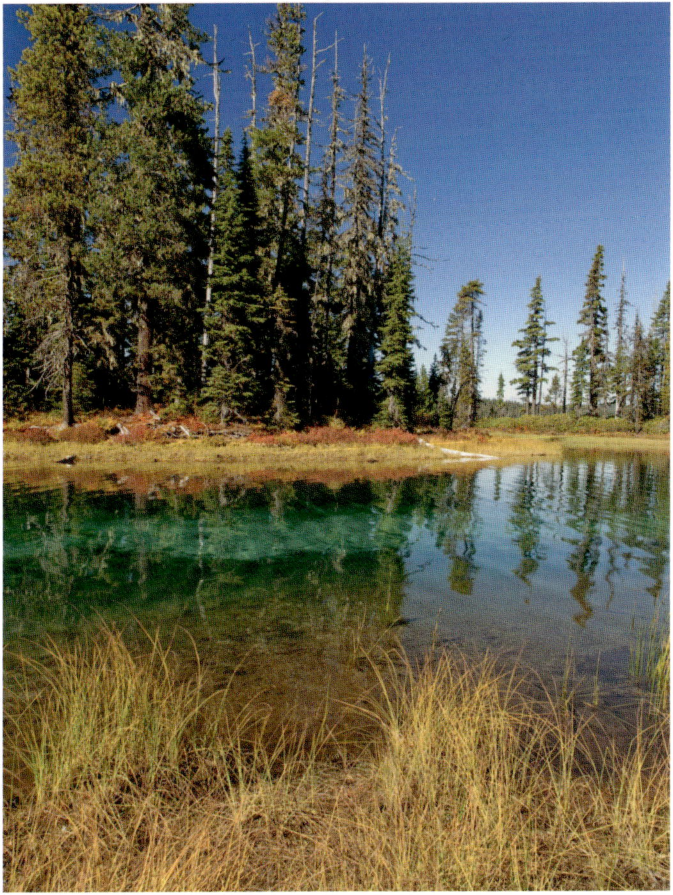

Waldo Lake, in the Cascade Mountains, is the second-deepest lake in Oregon after Crater Lake. *Photo by Vivian McAleavey.*

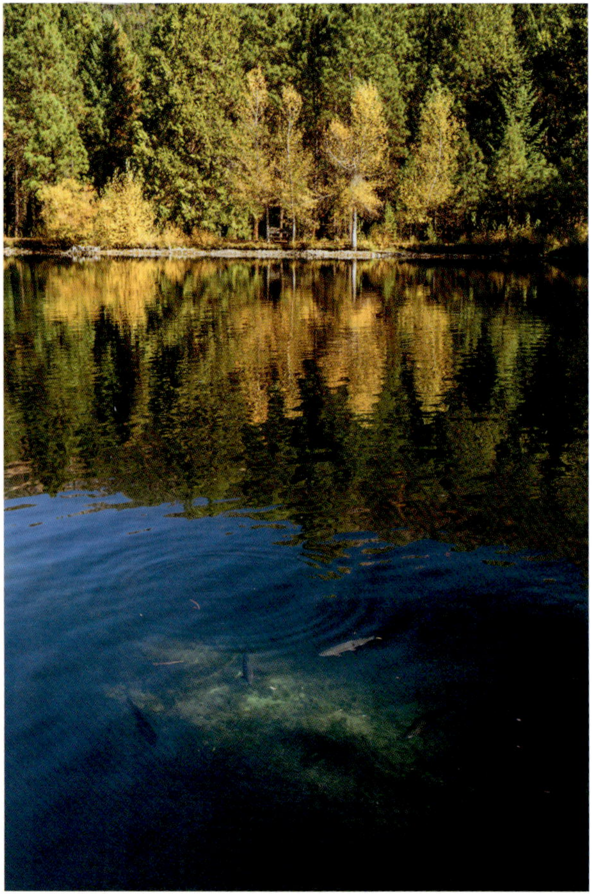

Wizard Falls Fish Hatchery in Sherman raises rainbow trout, kokanee salmon, spring chinook, and summer steelhead. *Photo by Jay Newman*

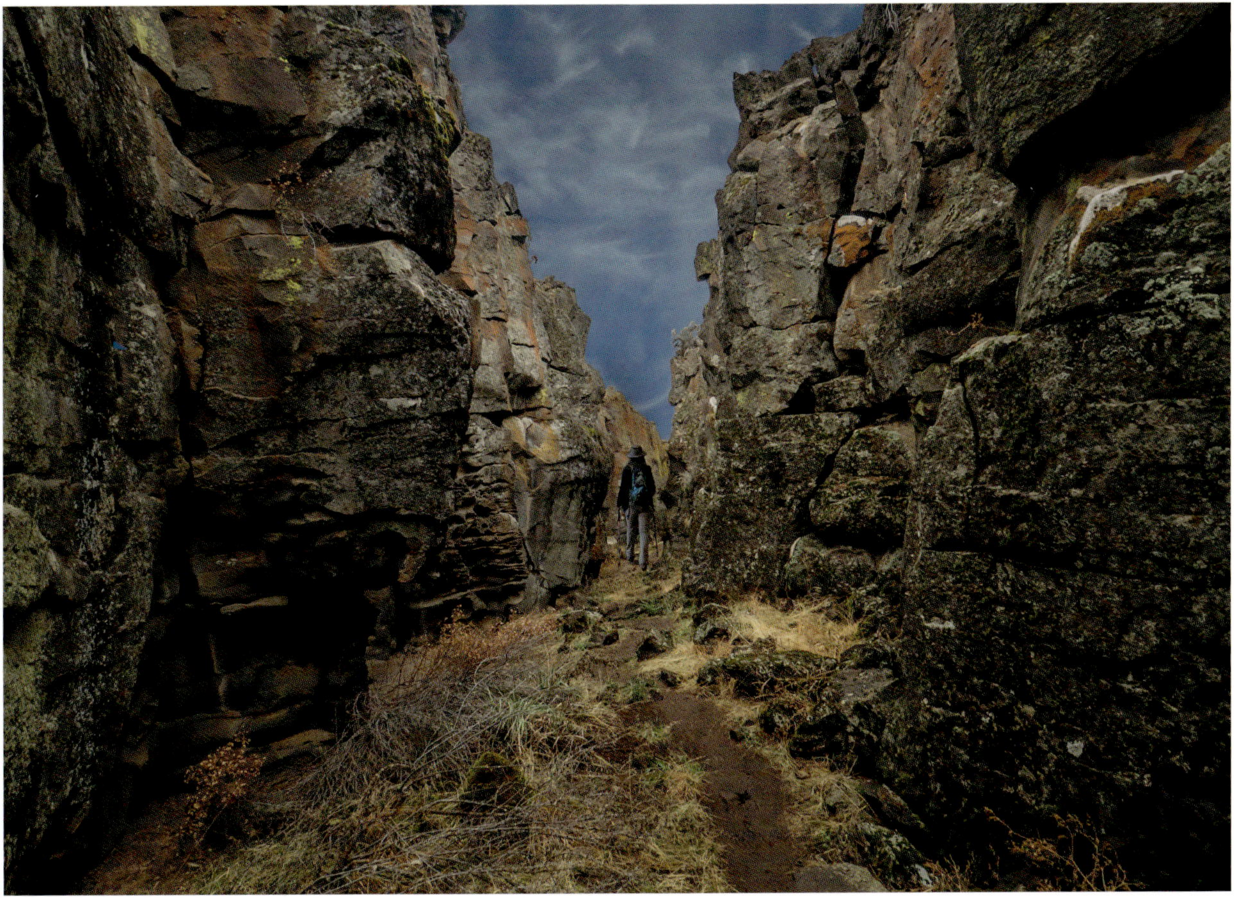

Crack in the Ground is in the Four Craters Lava Field in Christmas Valley. *Photo by Randy Bryan.*

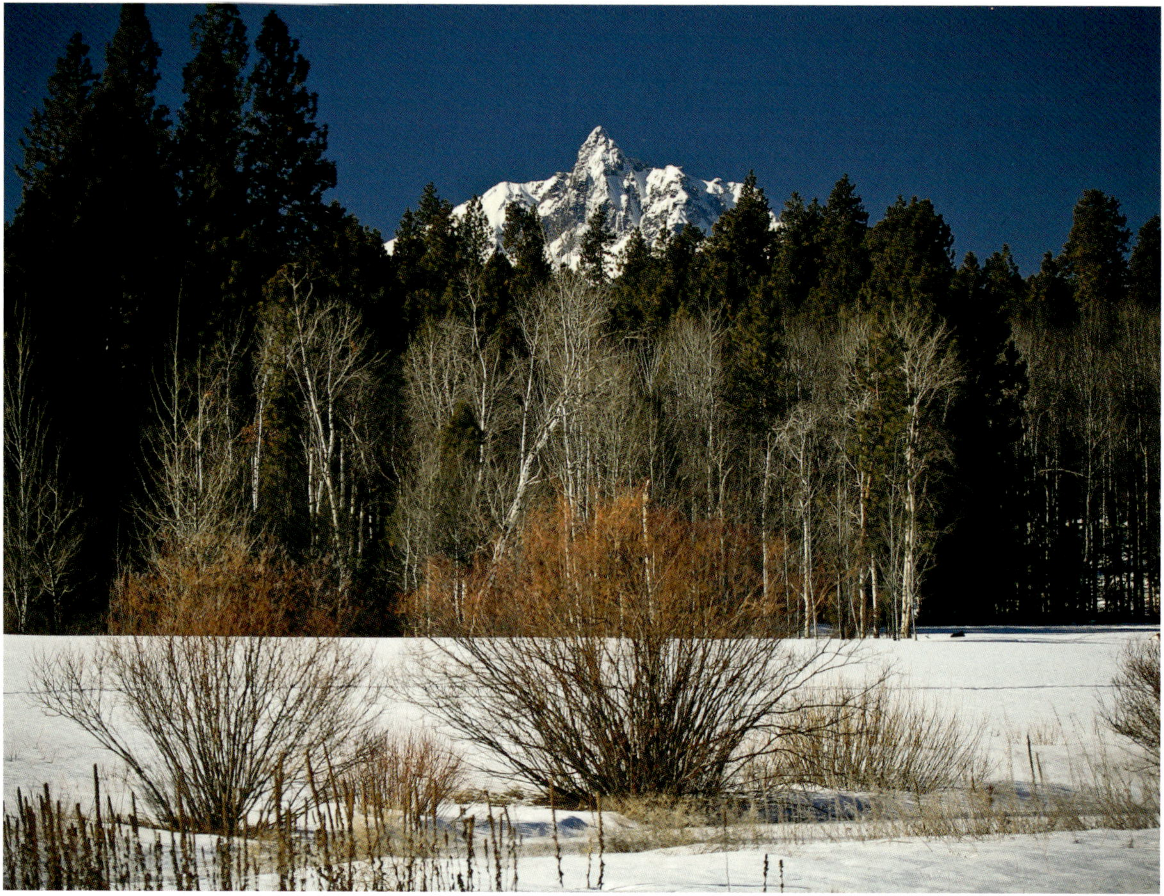

 Mount Washington from Black Butte Ranch. *Photo by Judy Benson LaNier.*

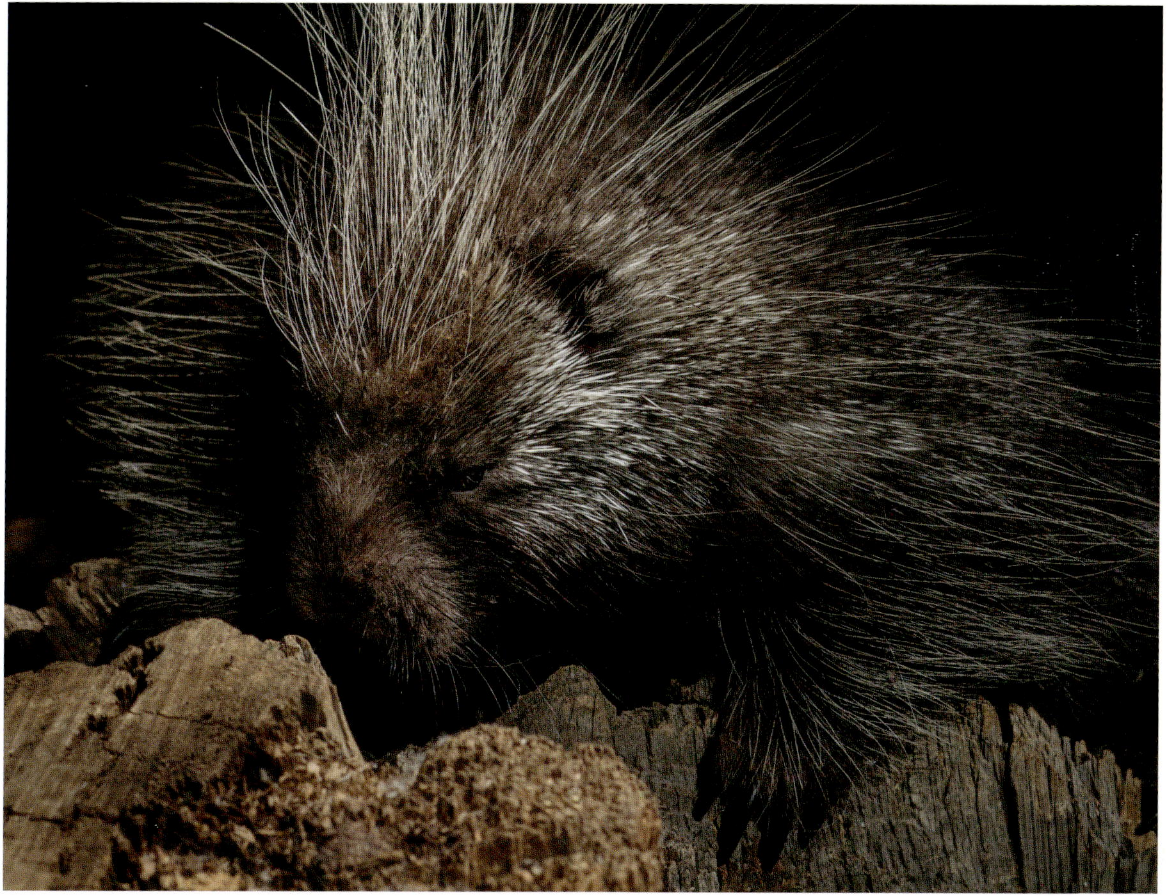

Porcupine at High Desert Museum, Bend. *Photo by Judy Benson LaNier.*

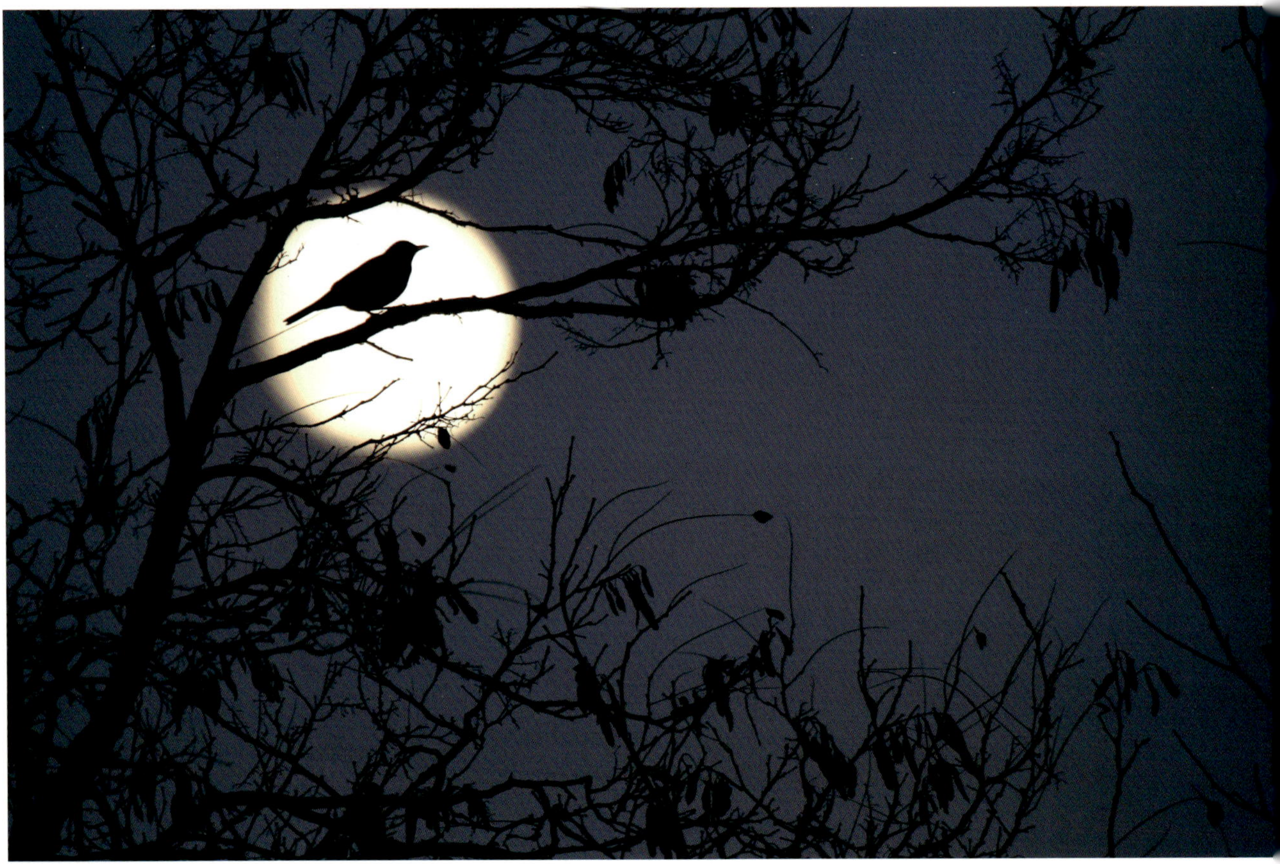

 Robin and moon. *Photo by Dan Elster.*

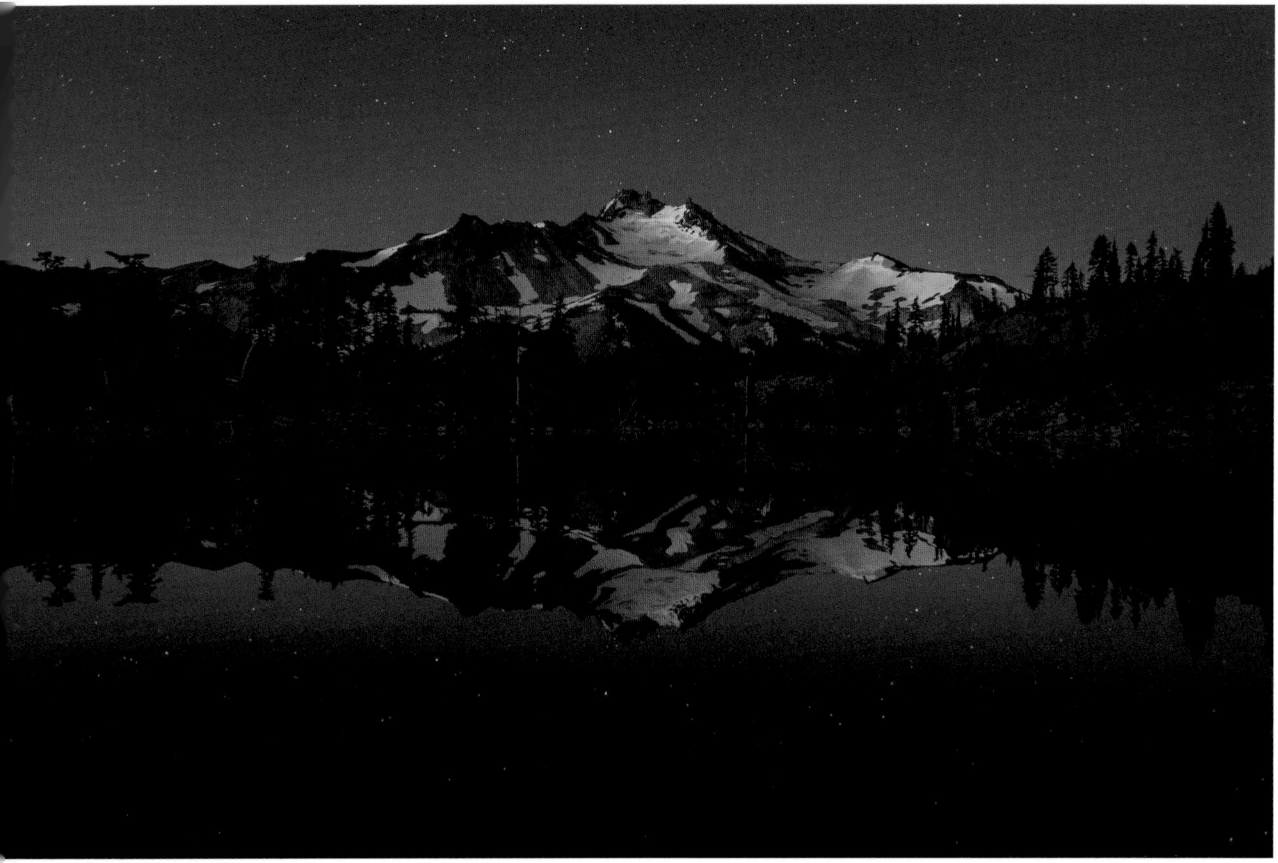

Mount Jefferson from Bay's Lake. *Photo by Vldn Taylor.*

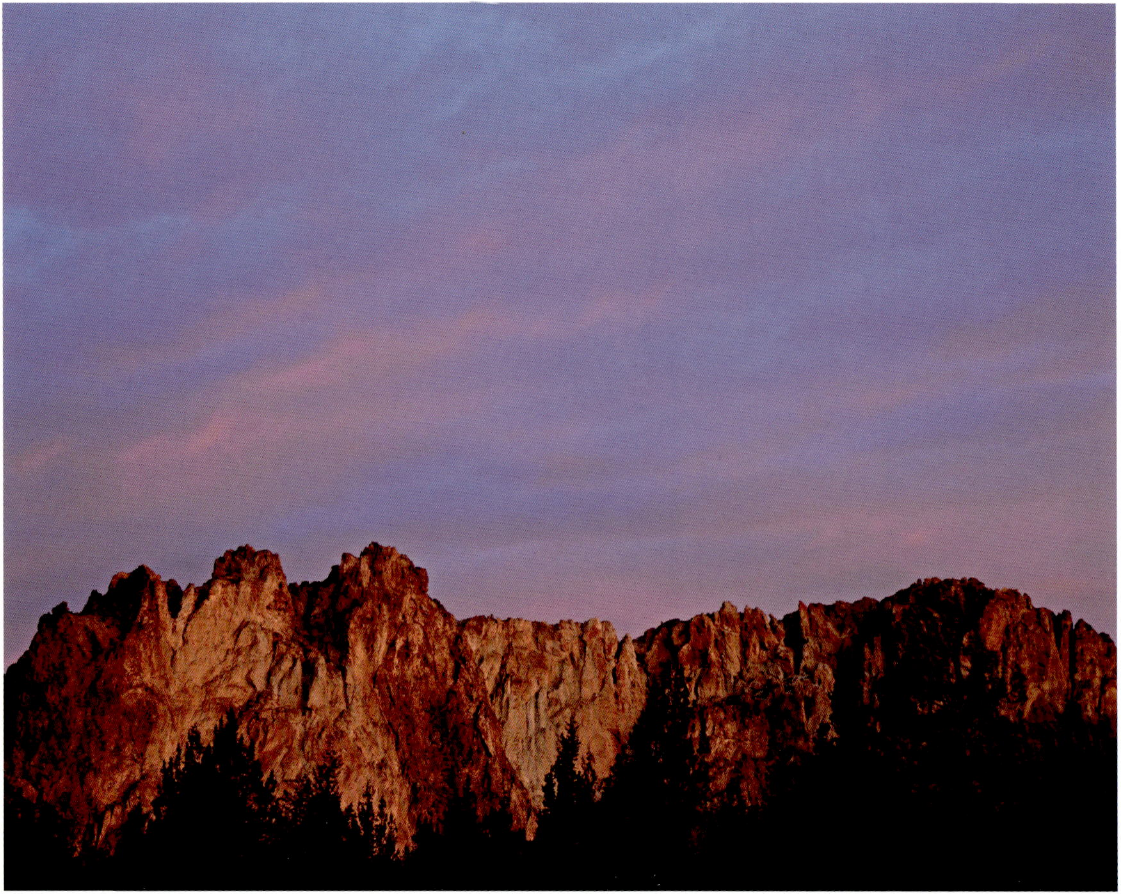

 Smith Rock. *Photo by Hans Stroo.*

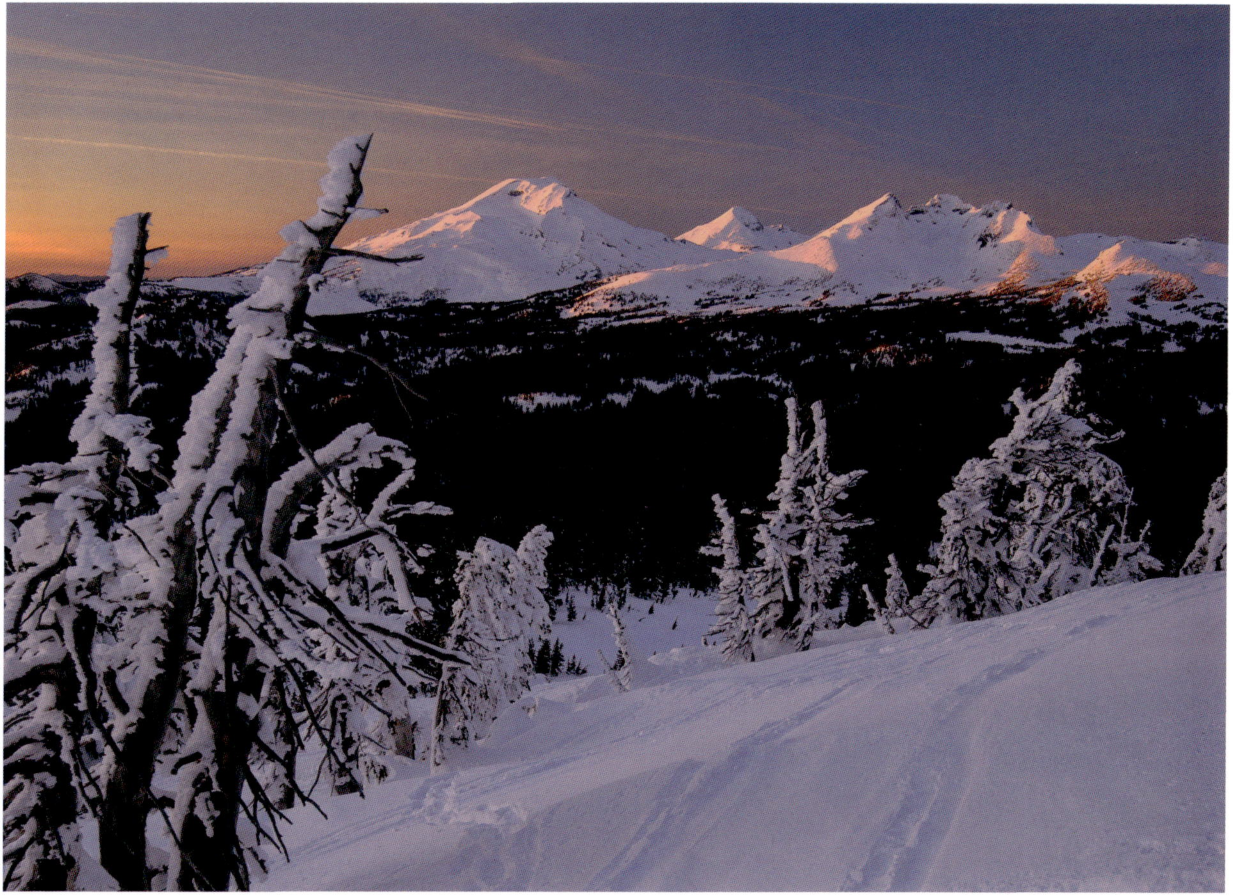

Three Sisters and Broken Top from Tumalo Mountain. *Photo by Clem Paslack.*

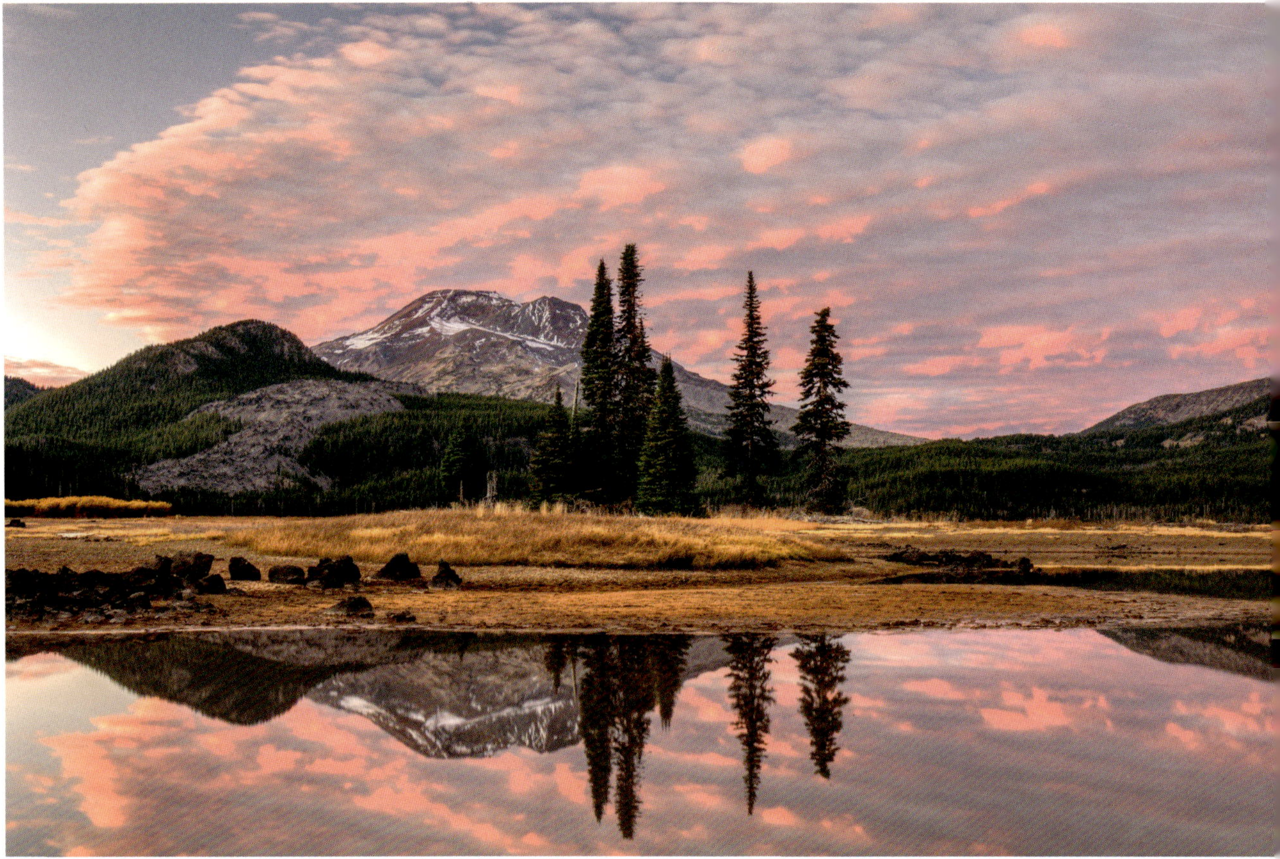

 Sparks Lake is twenty-five miles west of Bend. *Photo by Sue Newman.*

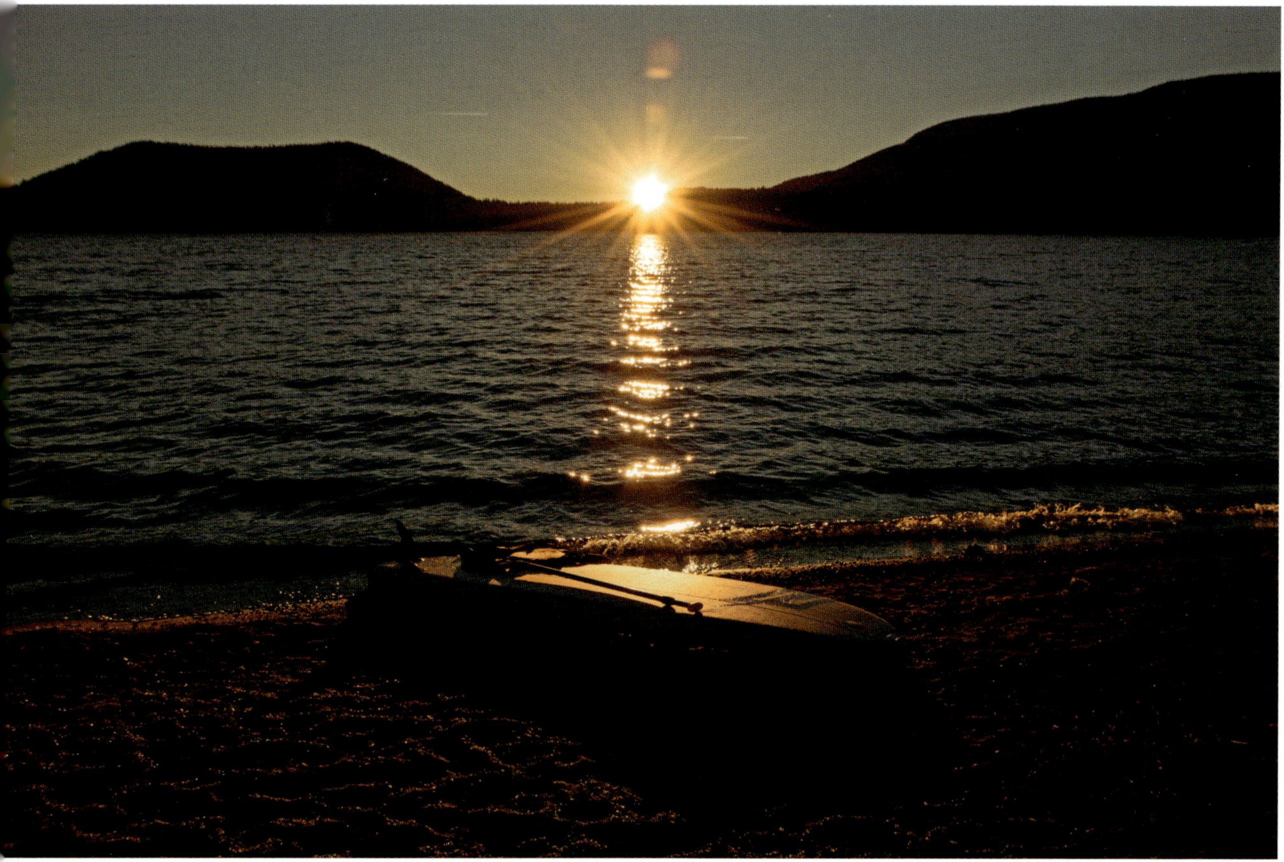

East Lake, part of Newberry Caldera, is in the Deschutes National Forest near La Pine. *Photo by Jay Newman.*

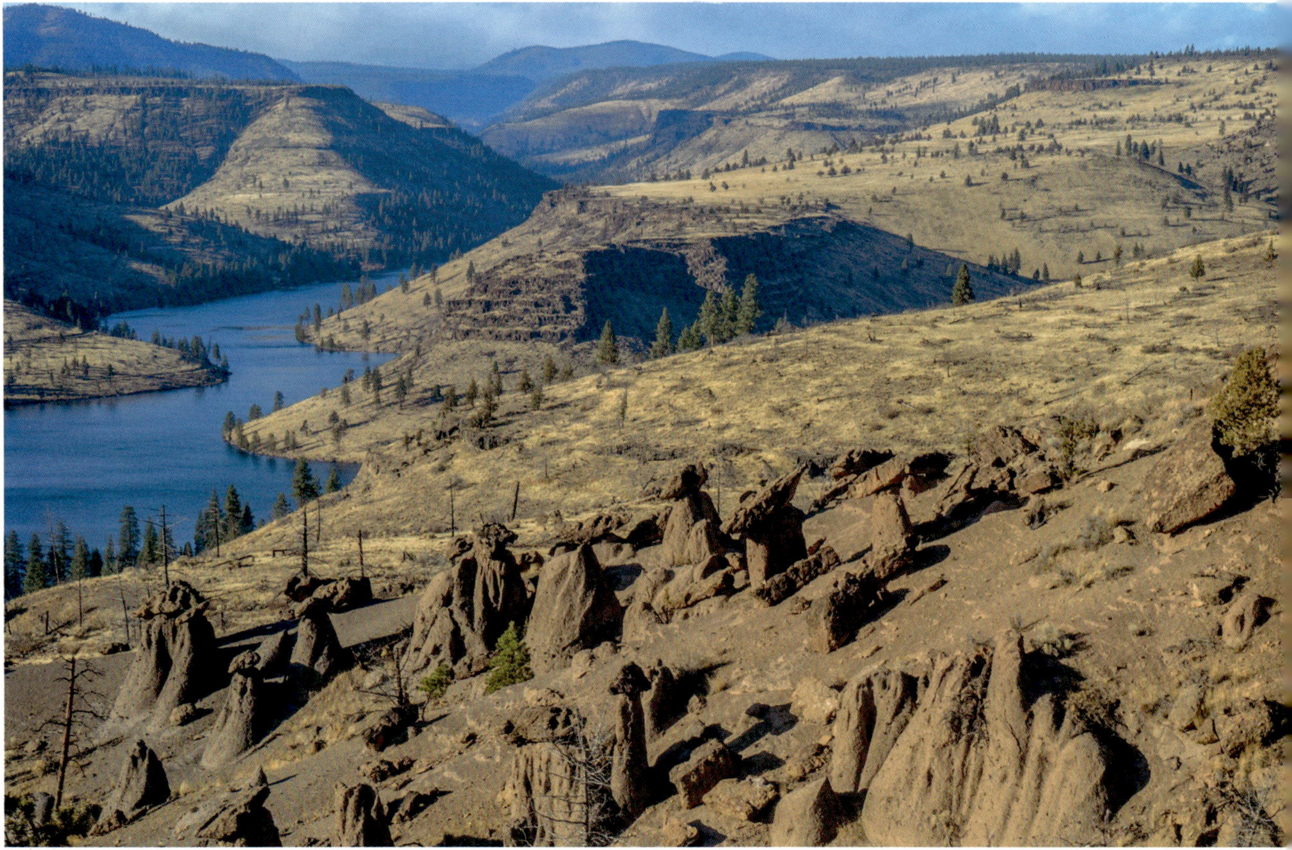

 Balancing Rocks are natural rock formations on the Metolius River near the Deschutes National Forest. *Photo by Randy Bryan.*

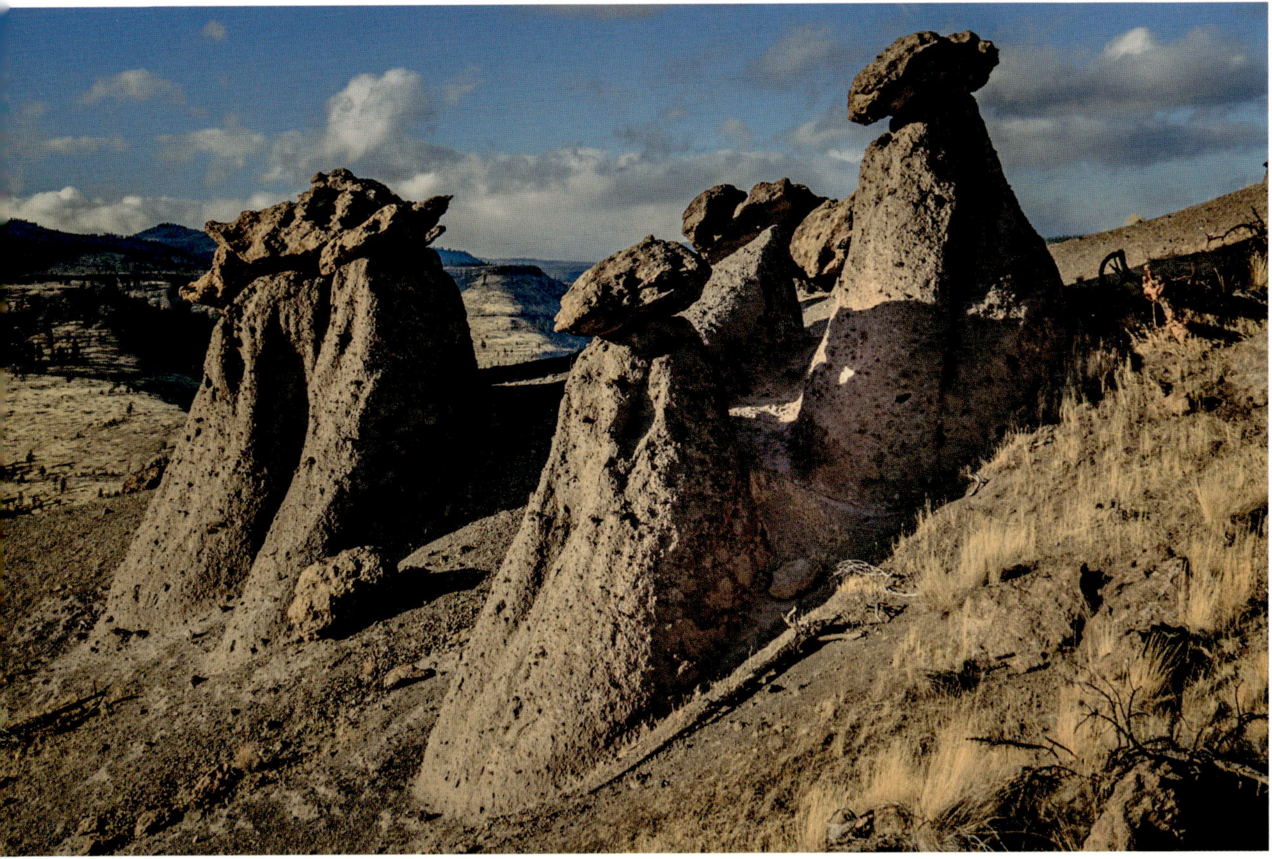

Balancing Rocks, near the Deschutes National Forest. *Photo by Randy Bryan.*

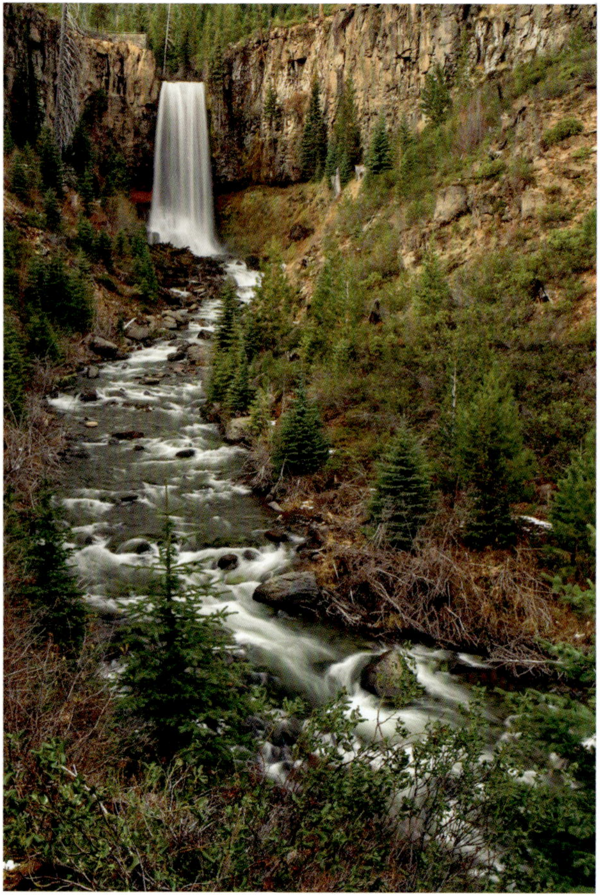

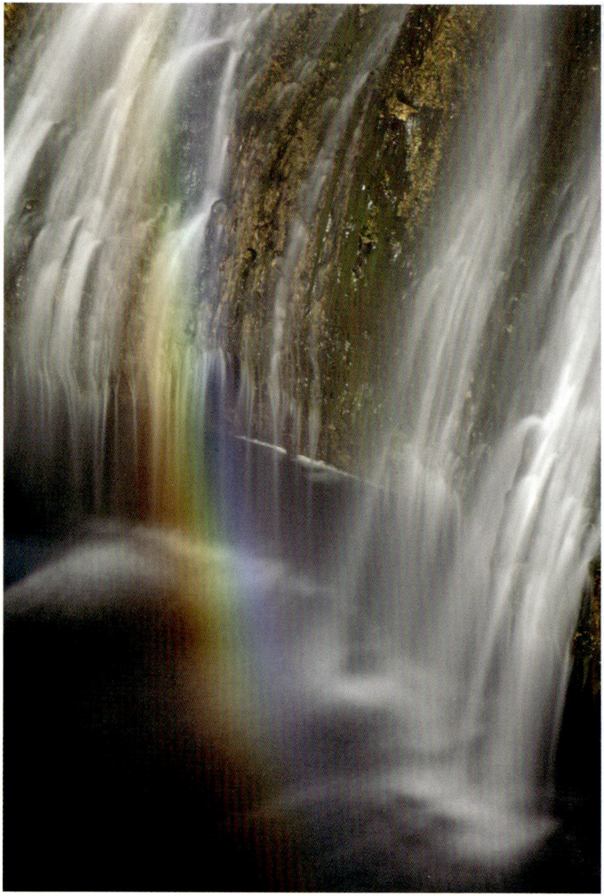

 Tumalo Falls is a 97-foot waterfall near Bend. *Photo by Jay Newman.* • Paulina Falls, Newberry National Volcanic Monument. *Photo by Jay New*

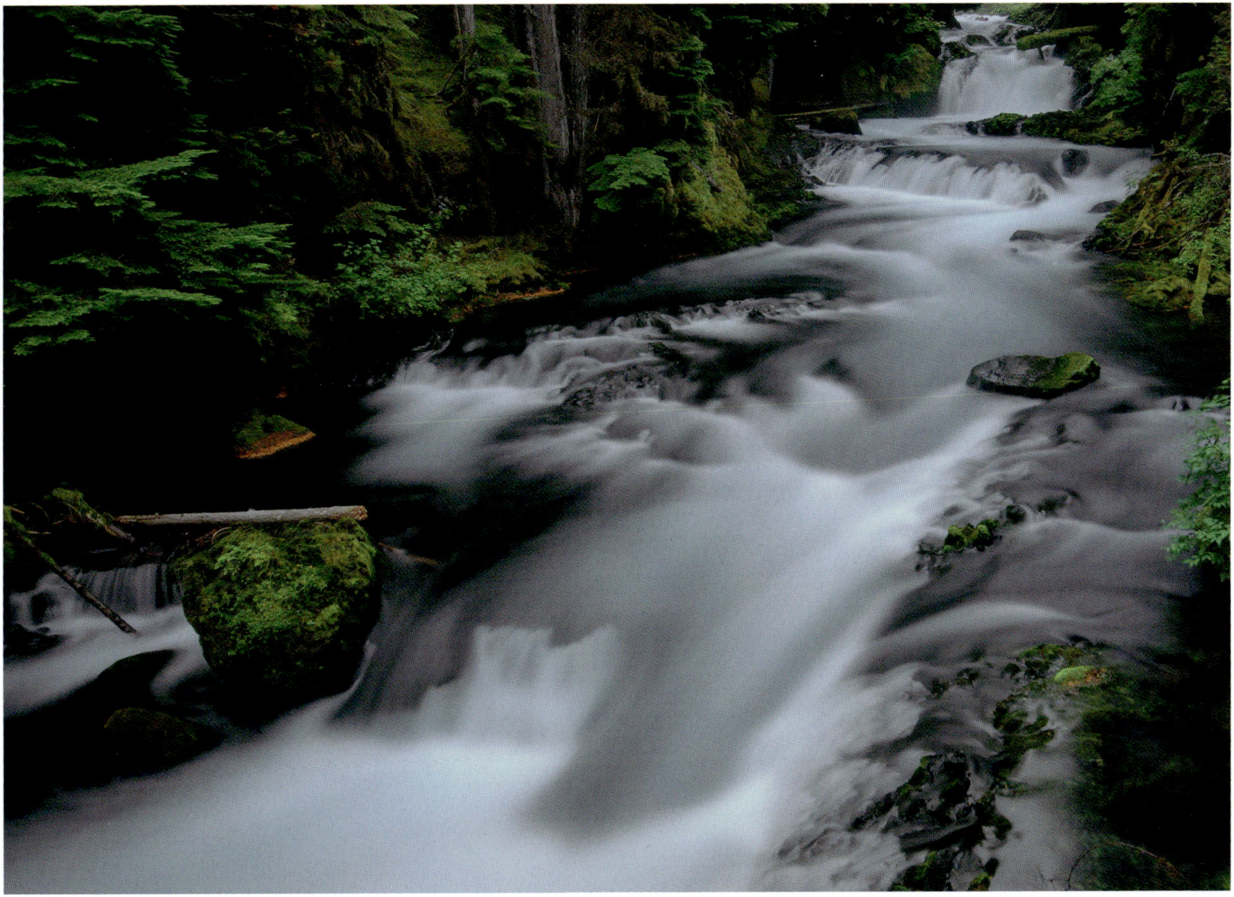

McKenzie River. *Photo by Clem Paslack.*

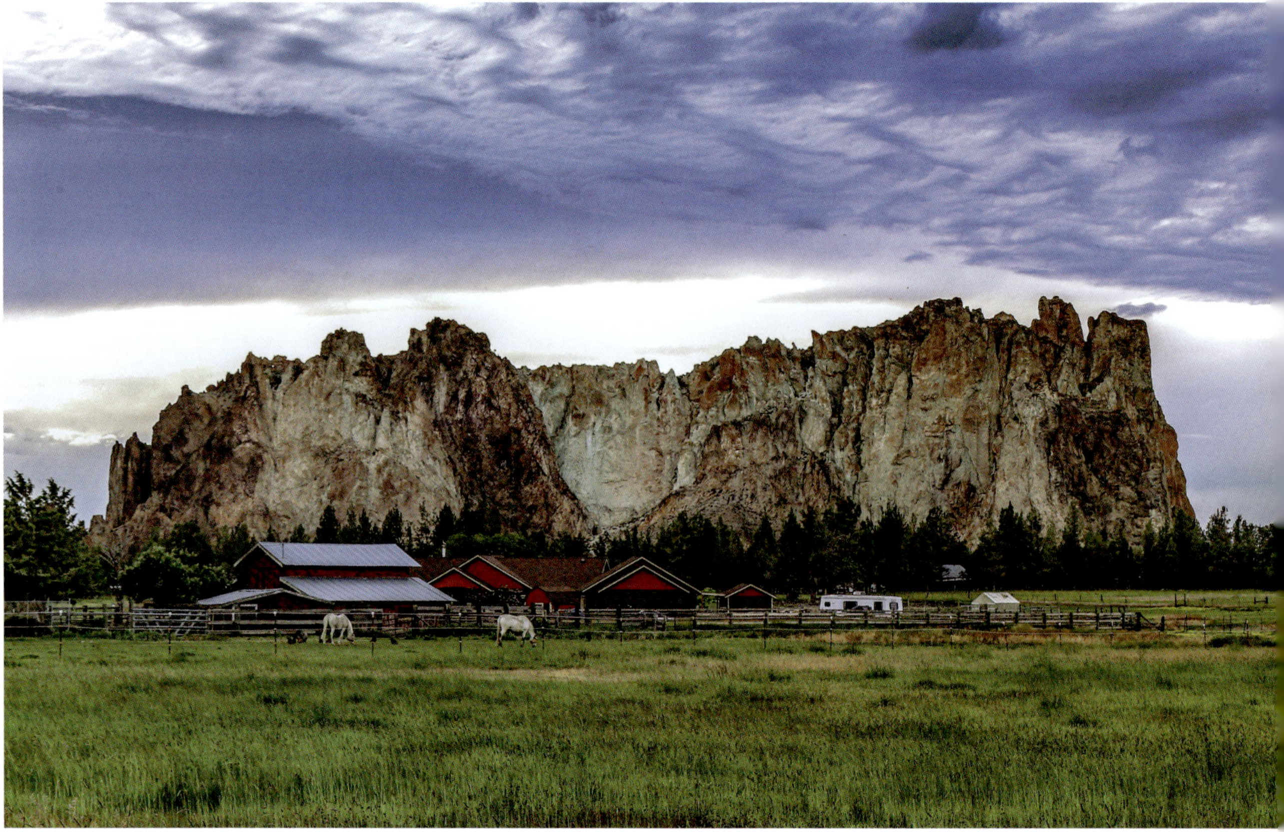

 Smith Rock State Park. *Photo by Terry Fisher.*

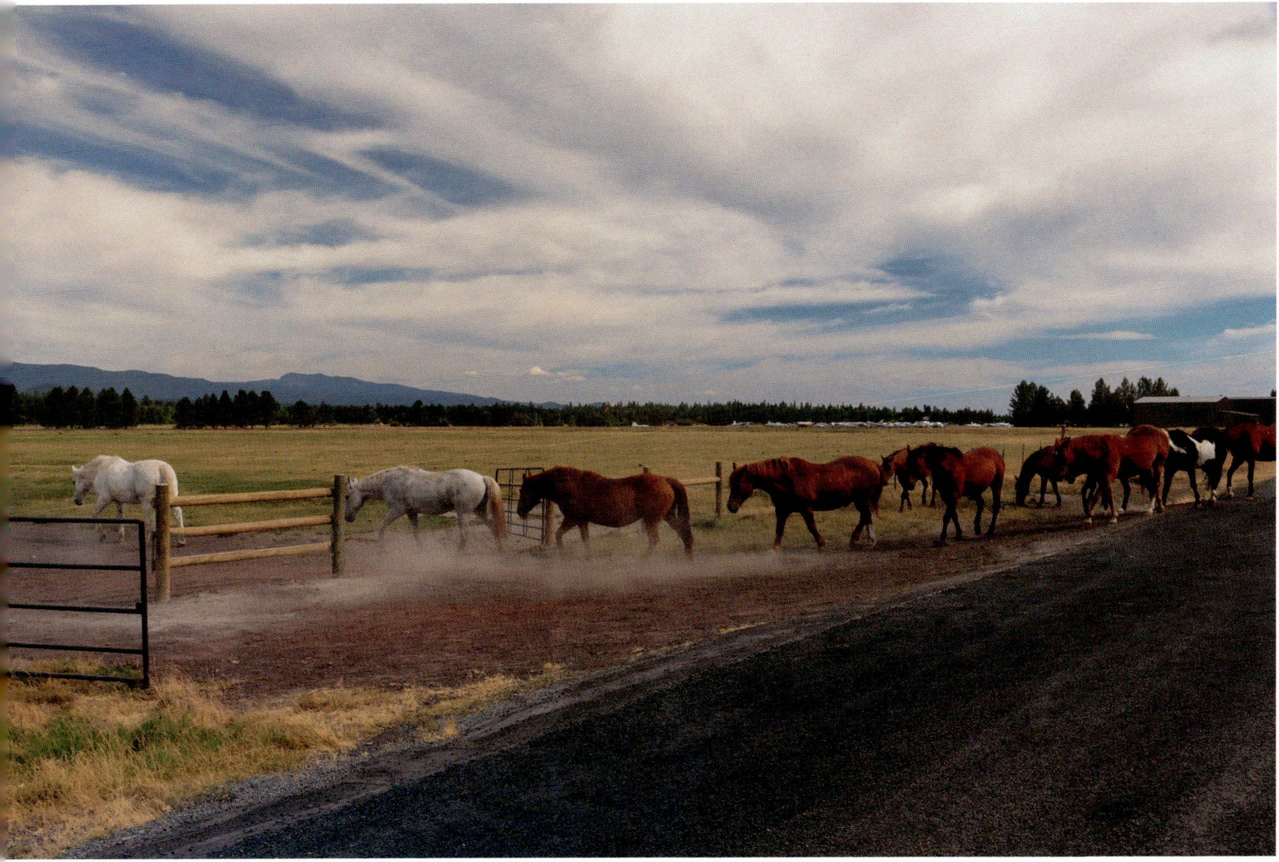

Sunriver horses. After a day of trail riding, these horses are headed to pasture. *Photo by Barbara Tricarico.*

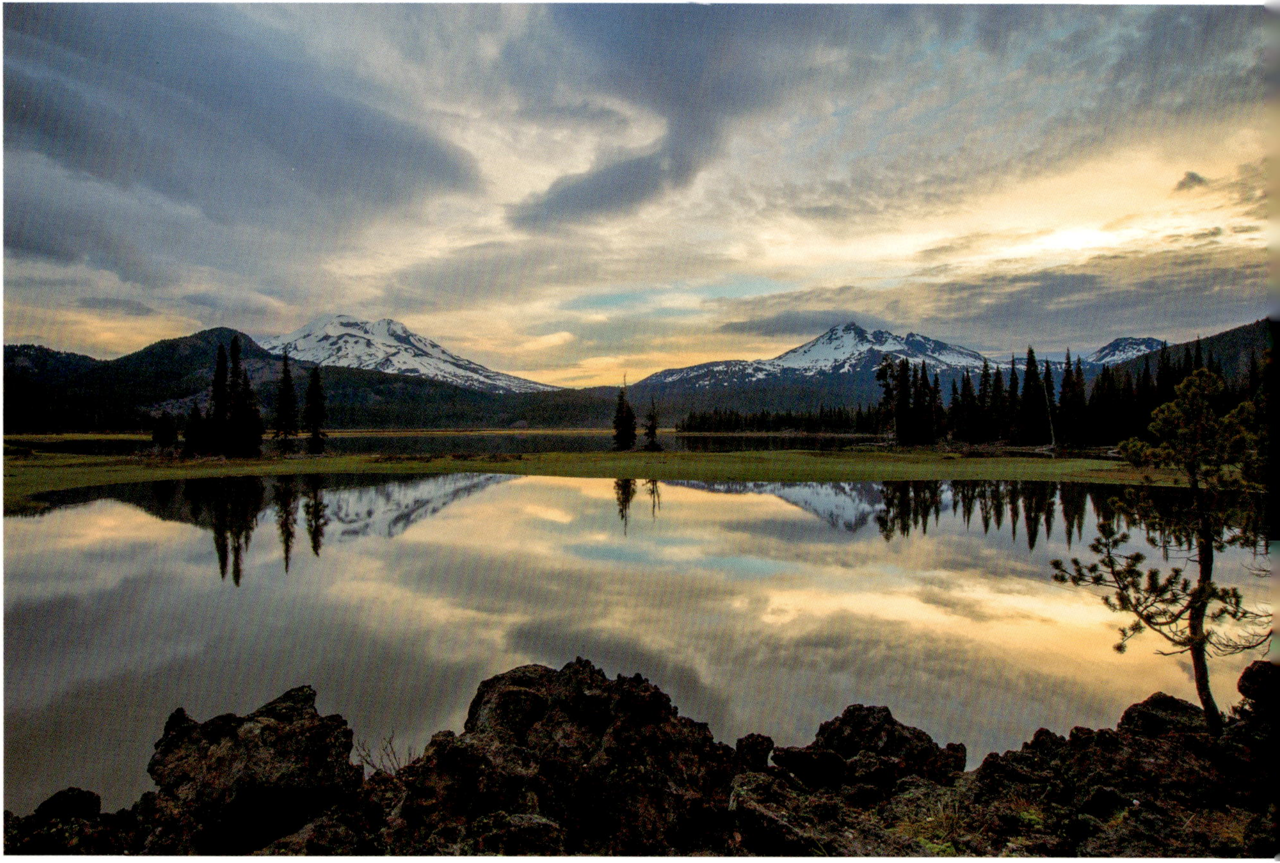

 Sparks Lake. *Photo by Vldn Taylor.*

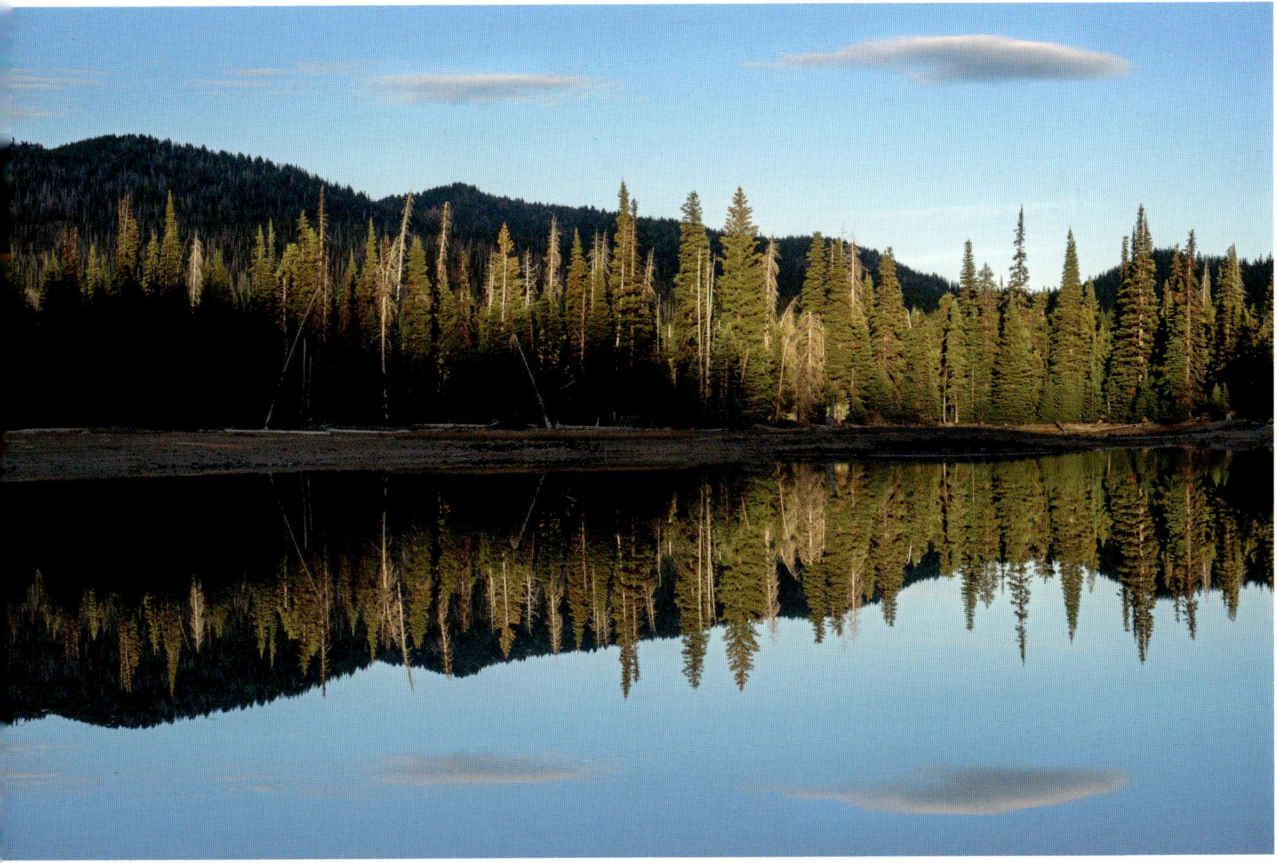

Sparks Lake reflection. *Photo by Jay Newman.*

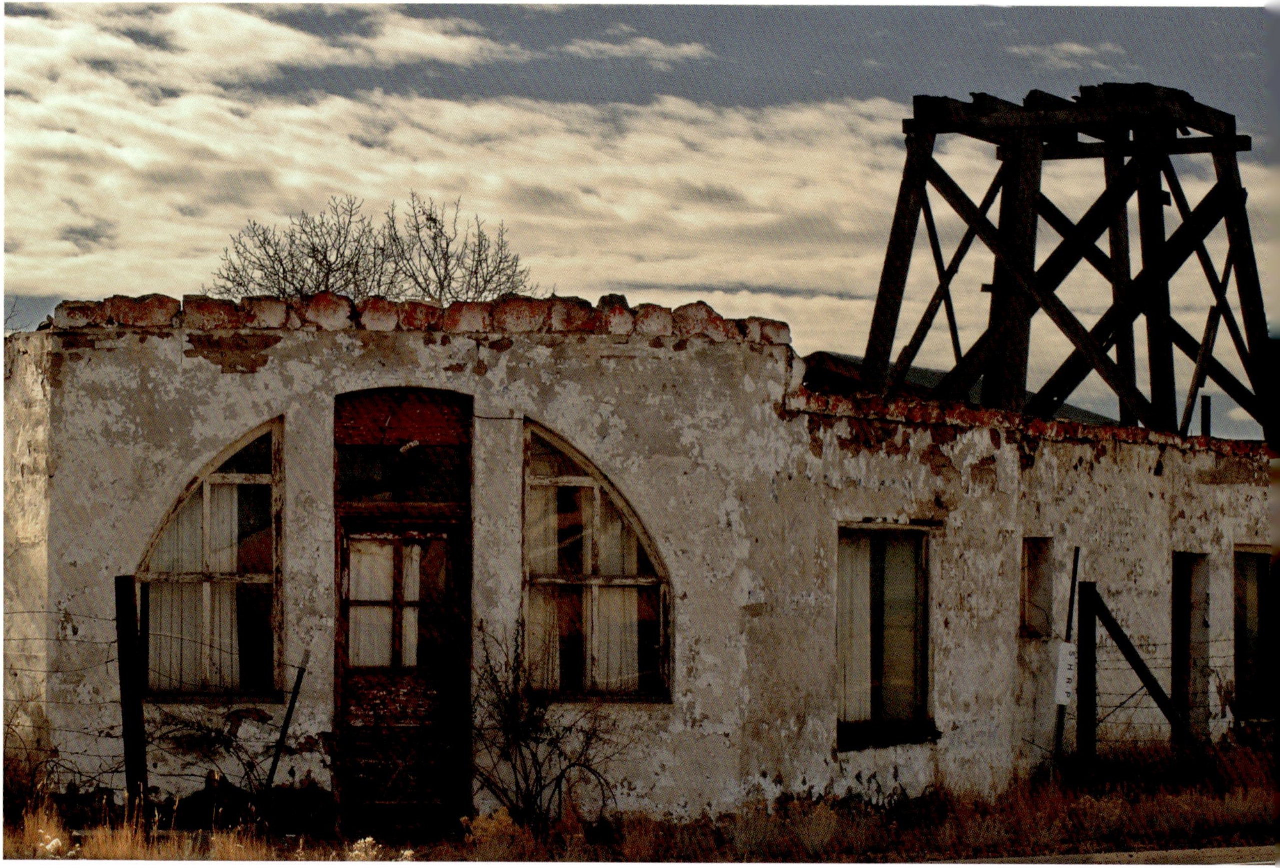

Abandoned building in Brothers. *Photo by Jay Newman.*

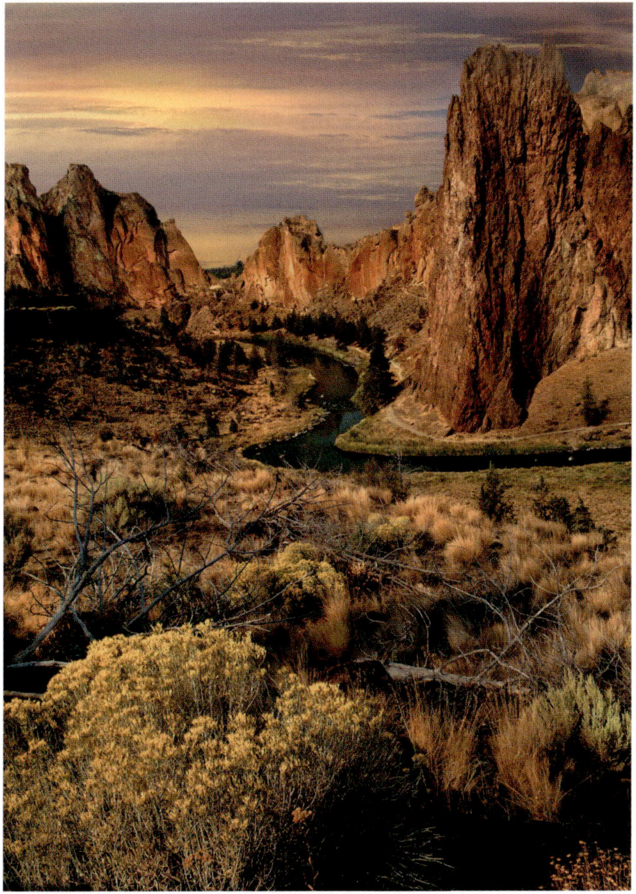

Smith Rock and Crooked River. *Photo by Neal R. Thompson.*

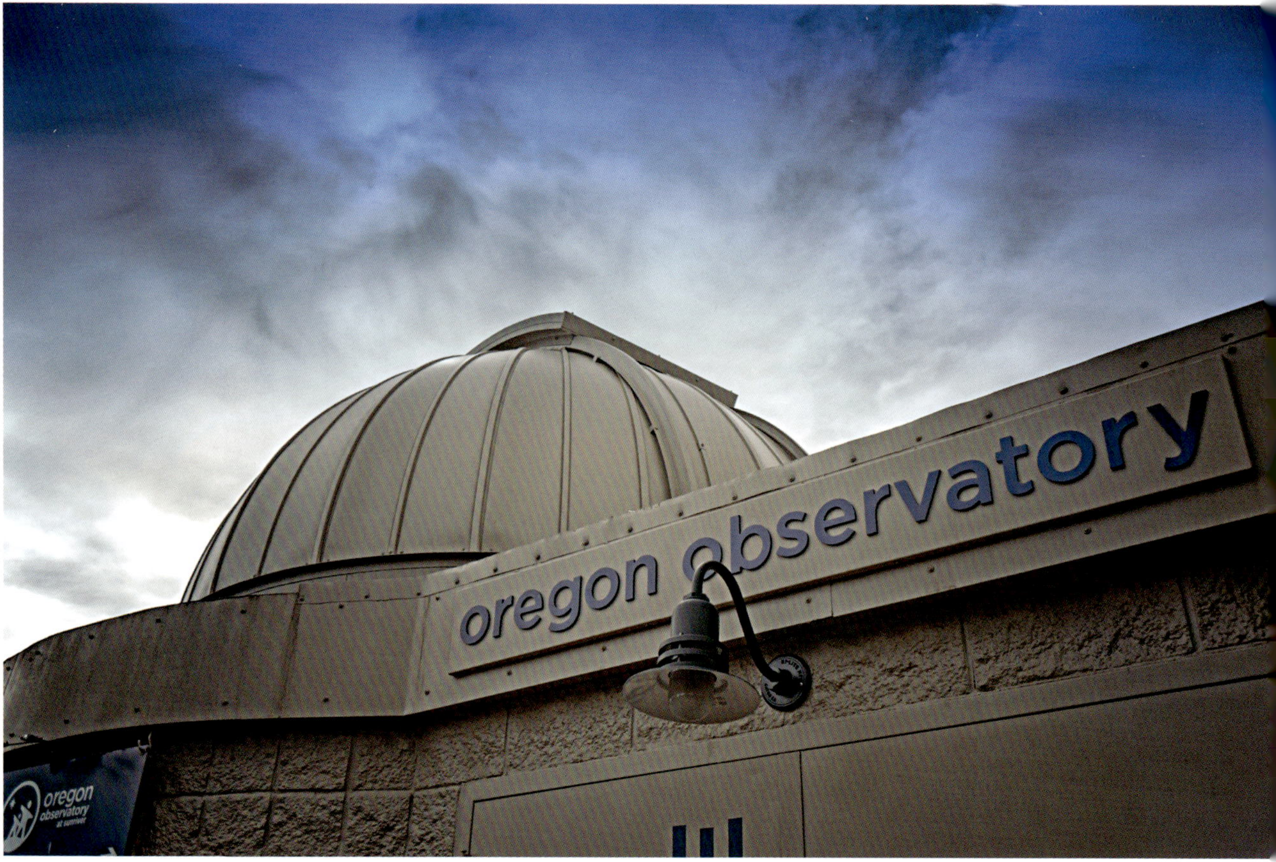

 Oregon Observatory at Sunriver. The astronomical observatory has eleven telescopes. *Photo by Barbara Tricarico.*

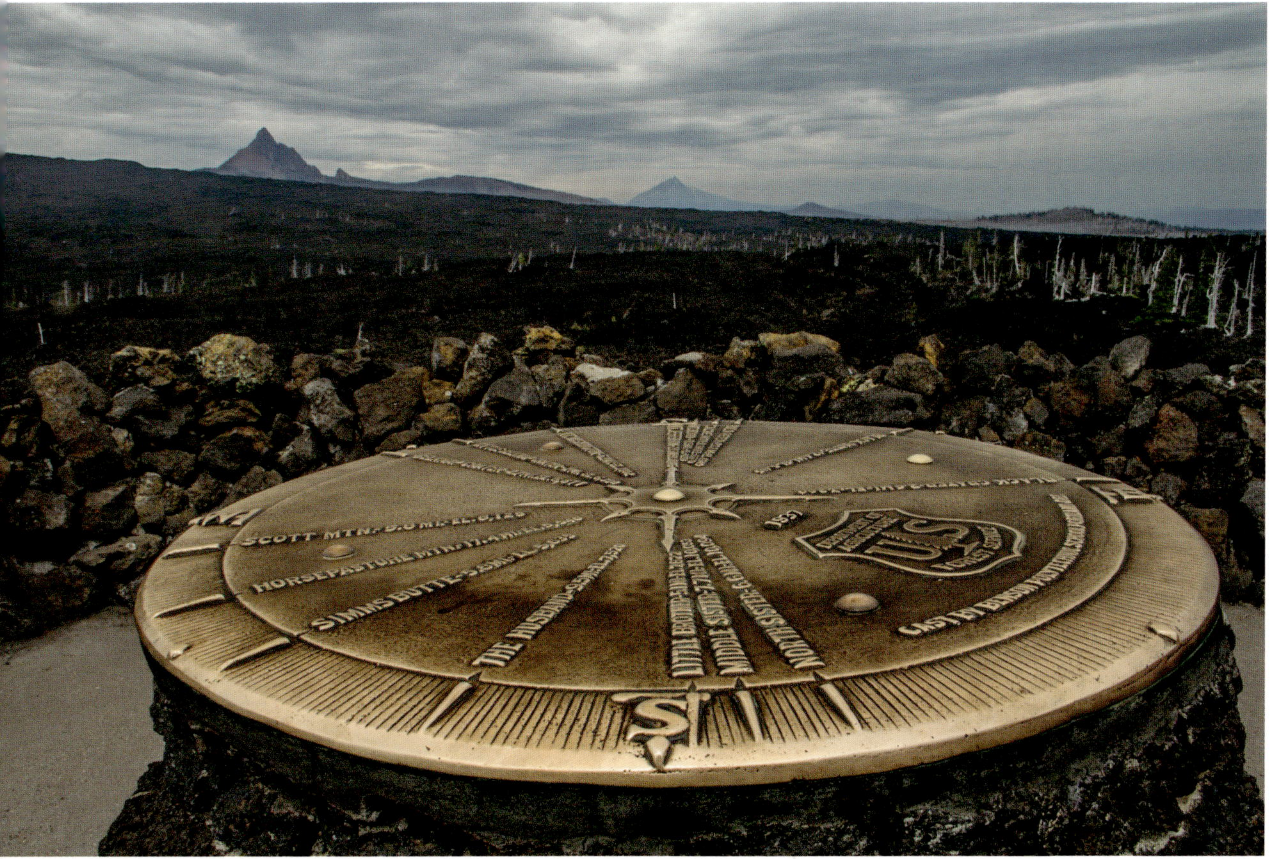

ee Wright Observatory pointer in the Deschutes National Forest at the McKenzie Pass. The Civilian Conservation Corps built the observa-
ory during the Great Depression, and it was completed in 1935. Mount Washington is in the background on the left. *Photo by Howard Hunt.*

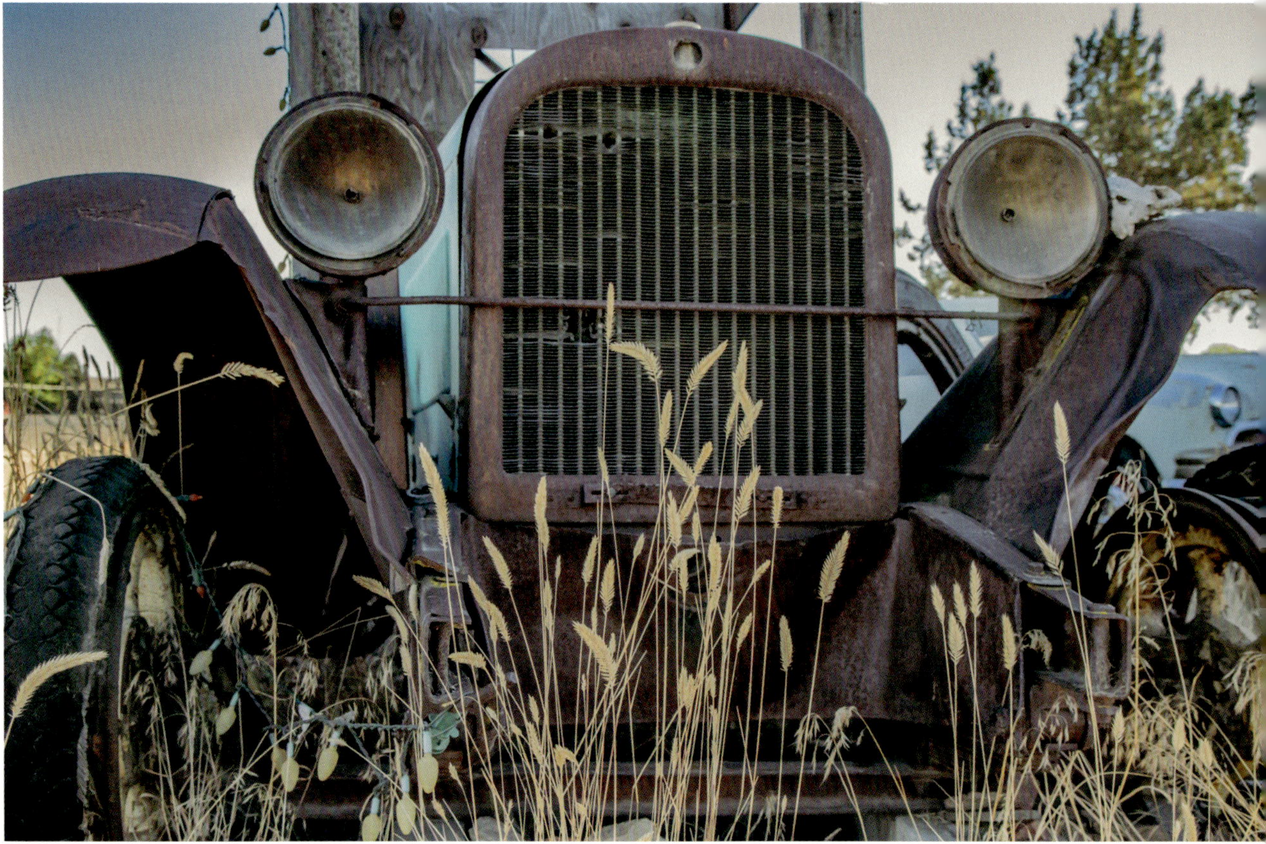

 Rusted antique near Madras. *Photo by George F. Peterson.*

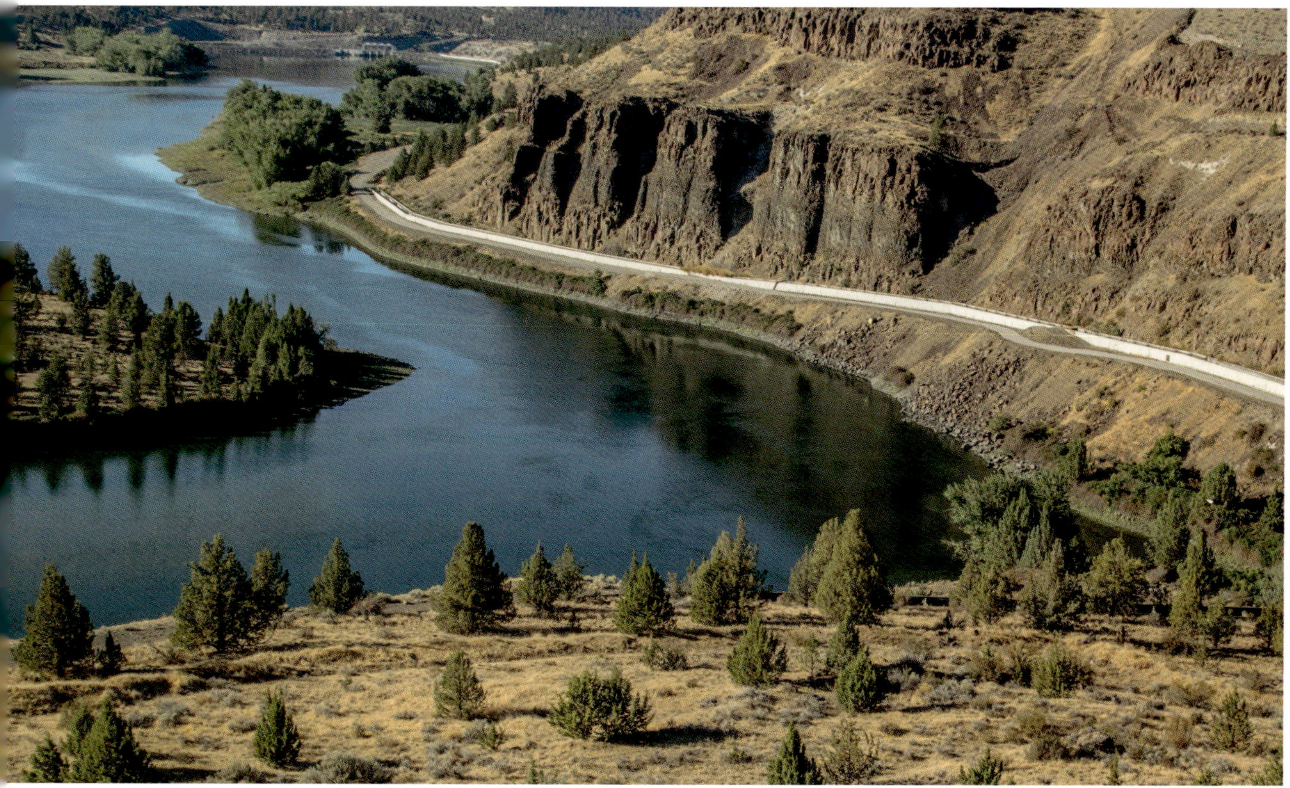

Warm Springs Reservation, near Madras. The area is occupied and governed by the Confederated Tribes of Warm Springs. *Photo by George F. Peterson.*

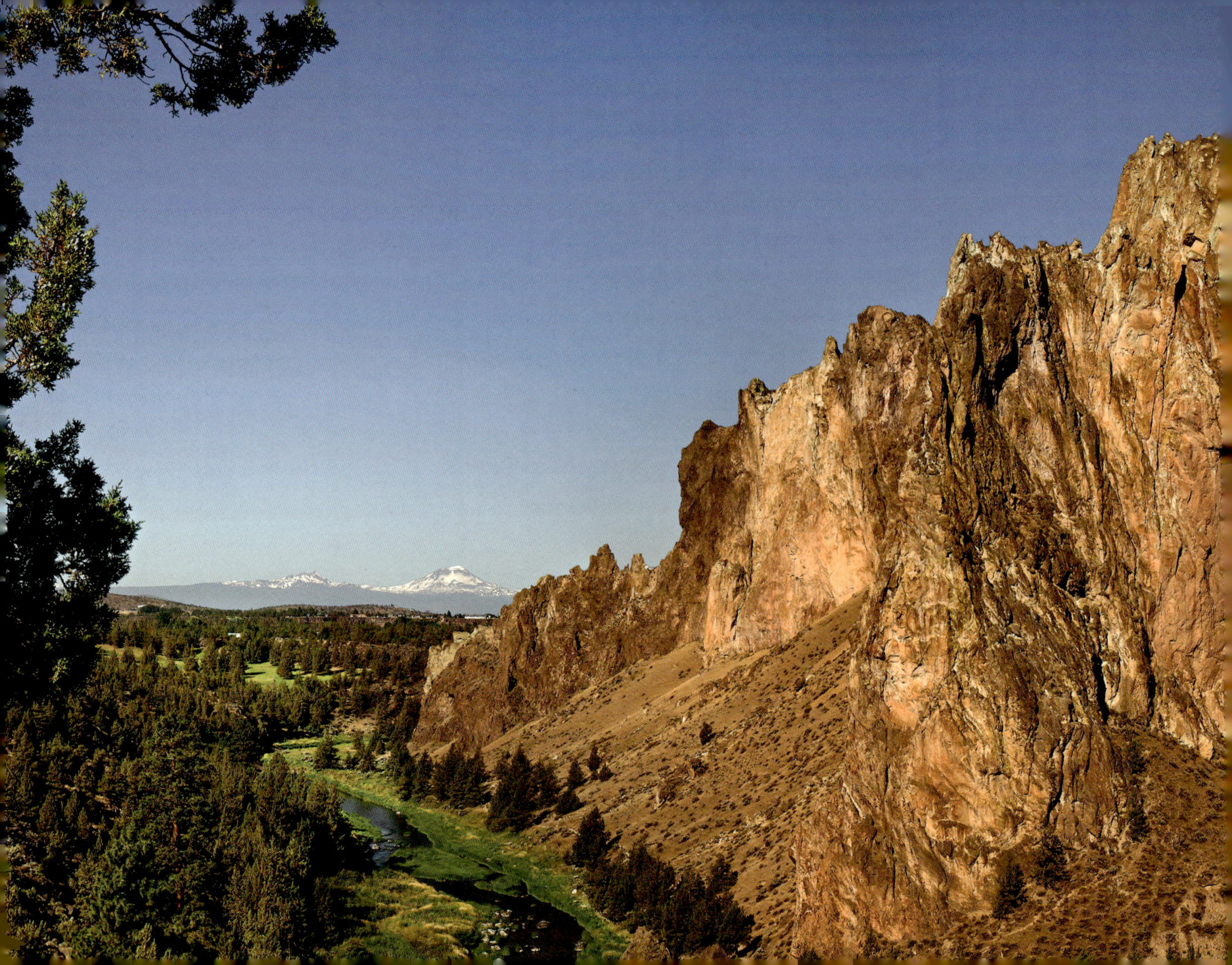

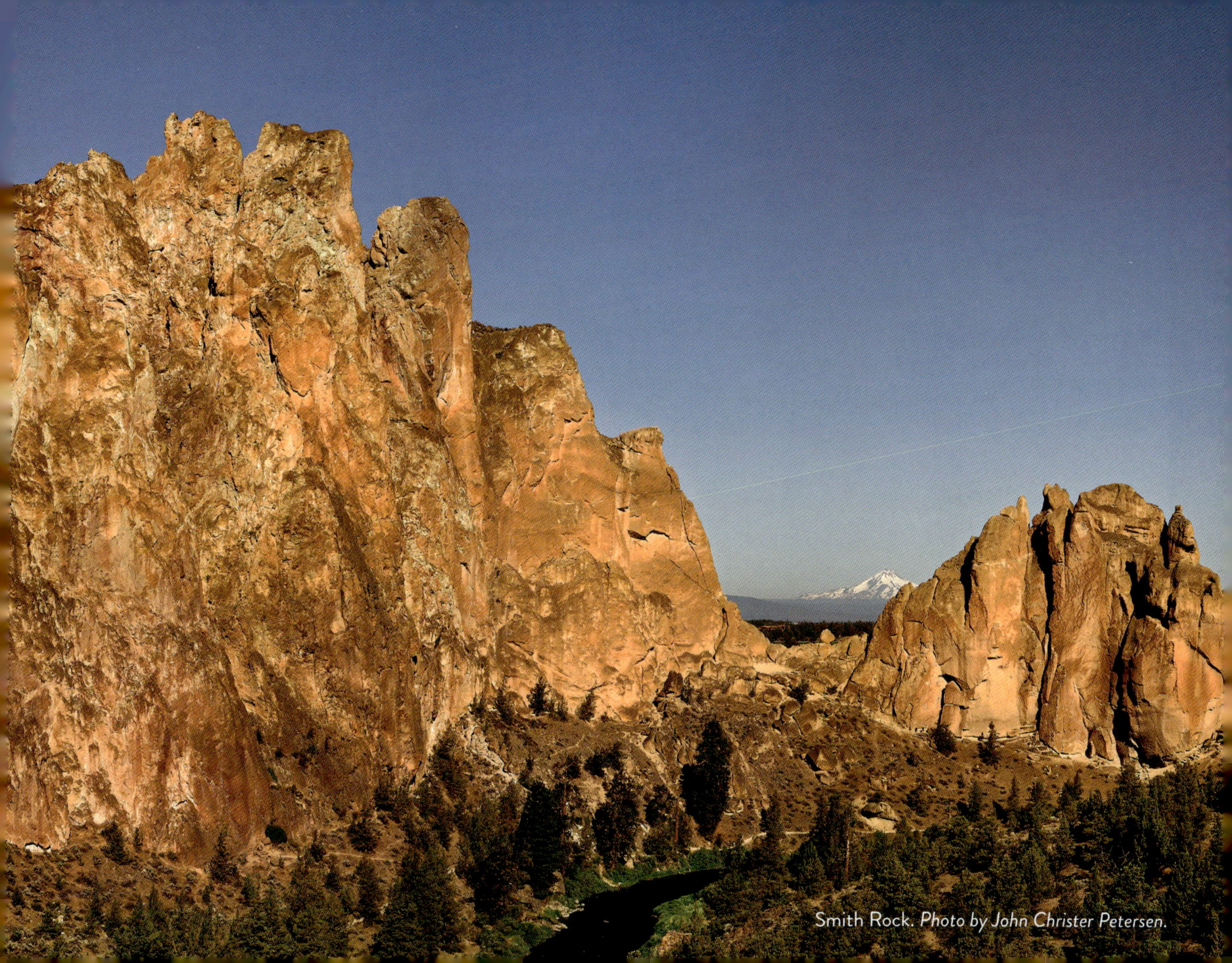

Smith Rock. *Photo by John Christer Petersen.*

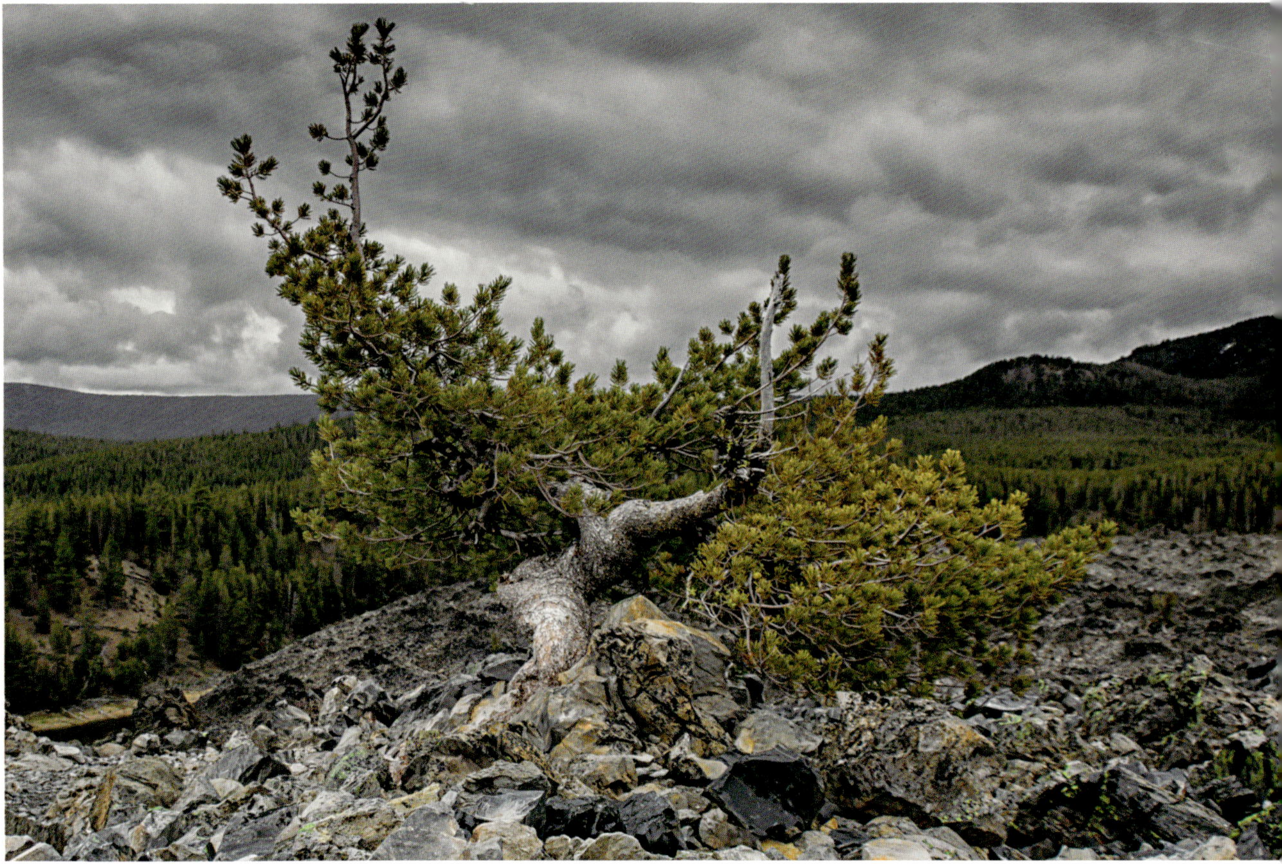

 Big Obsidian Flow, Newberry National Volcanic Monument. *Photo by Barbara Tricarico.*

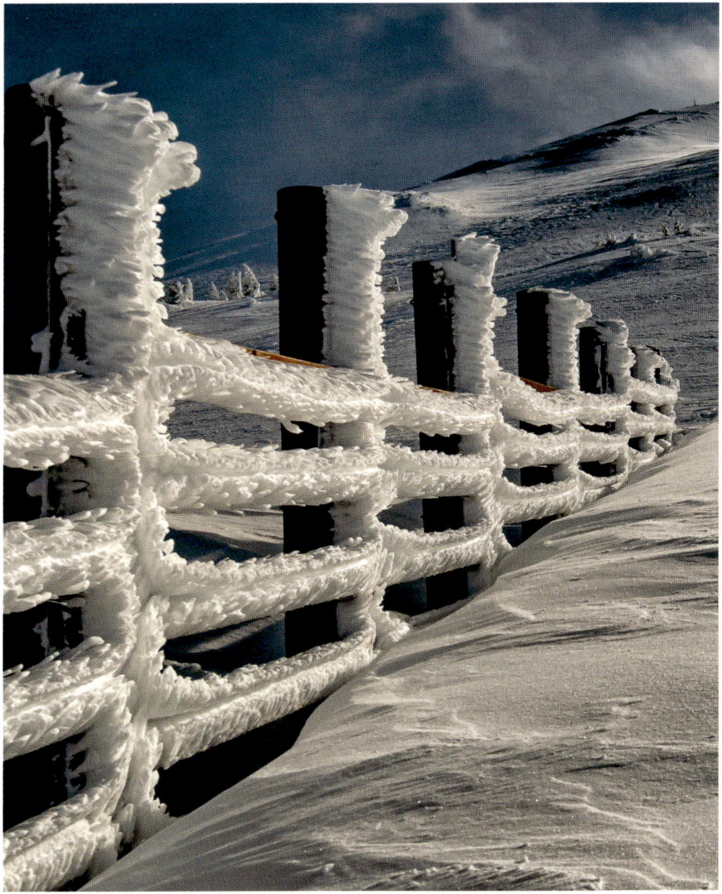

Frosted fence on Mount Bachelor. *Photo by Clem Paslack.*

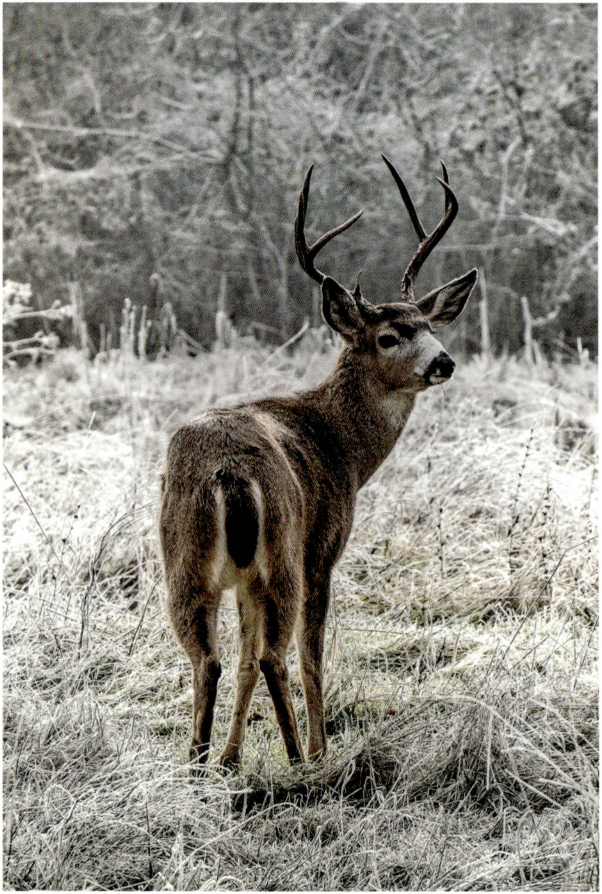

 Black-tailed buck. *Photo by Nick Viani.*

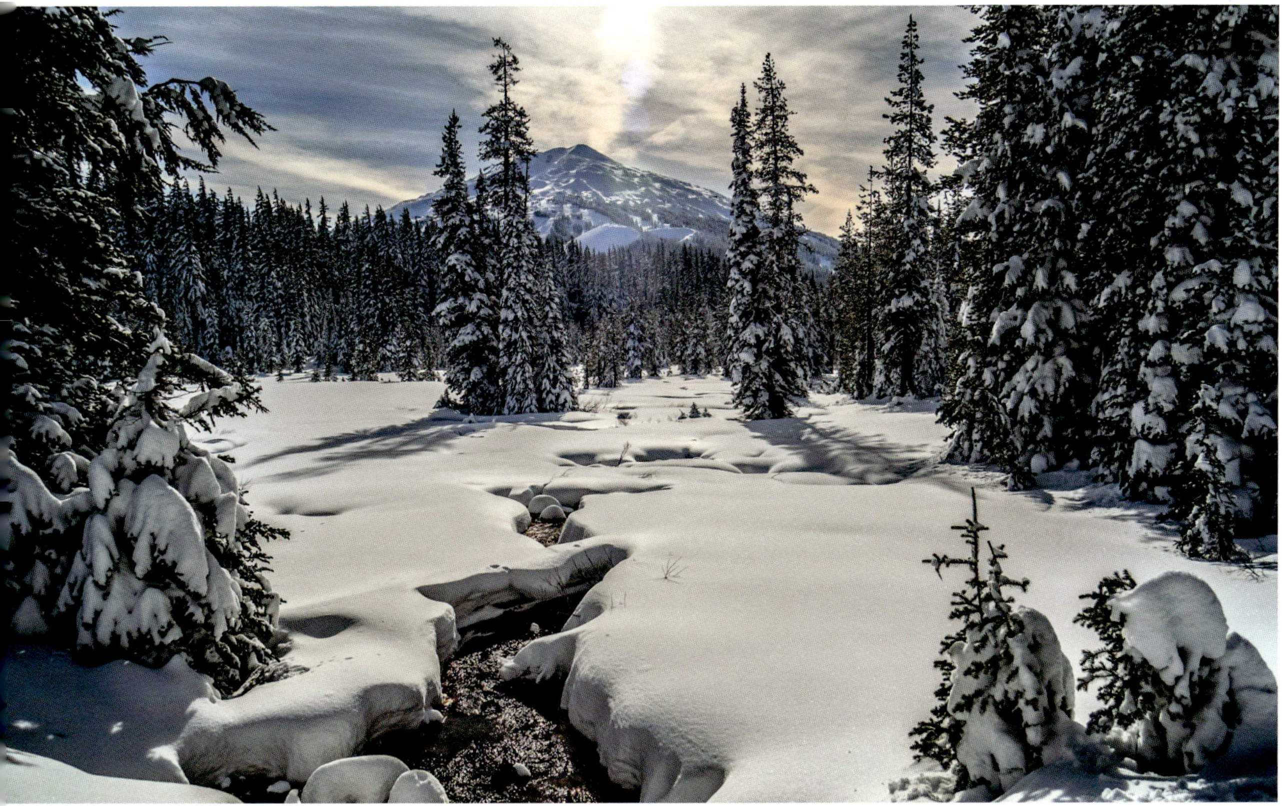

Mount Bachelor. *Photo by Randy Bryan.*

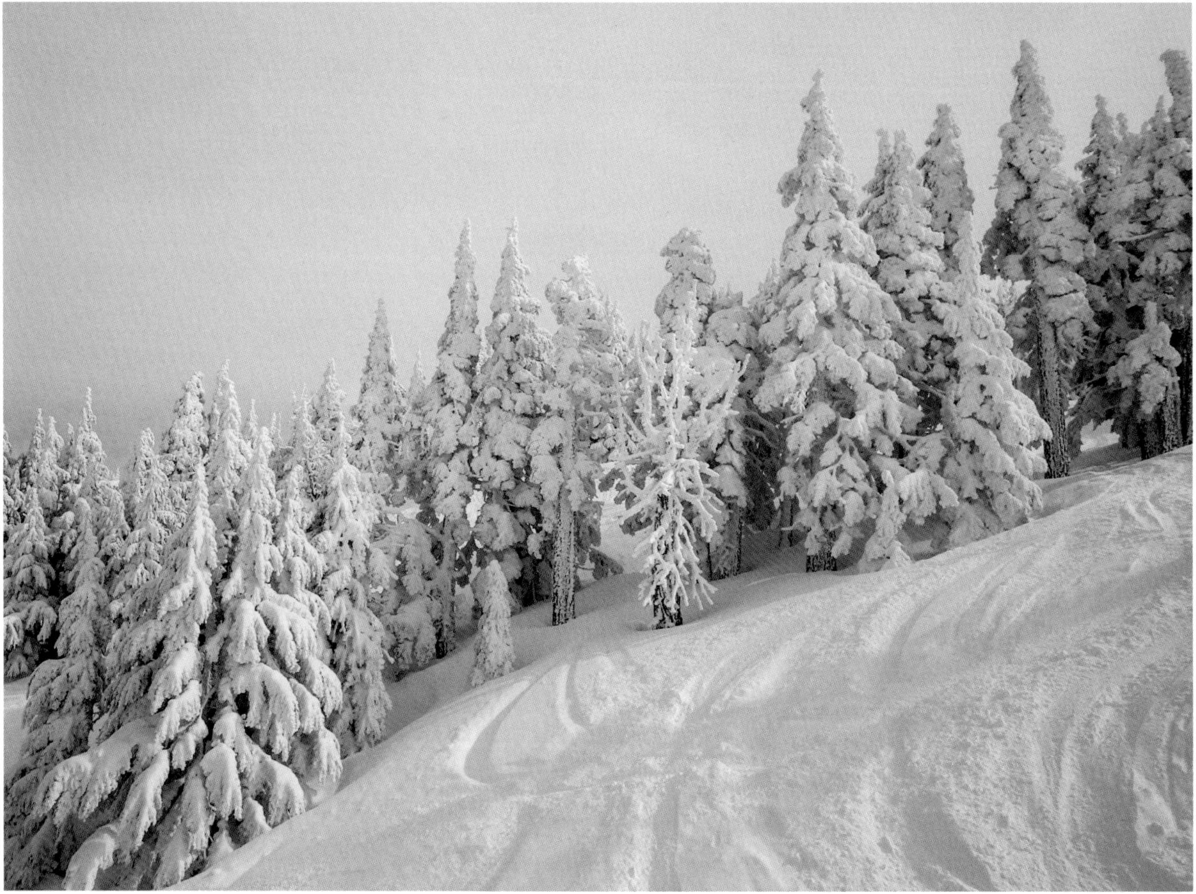

 Ski tracks in the snow, Mount Bachelor. *Photo by George F. Peterson.*

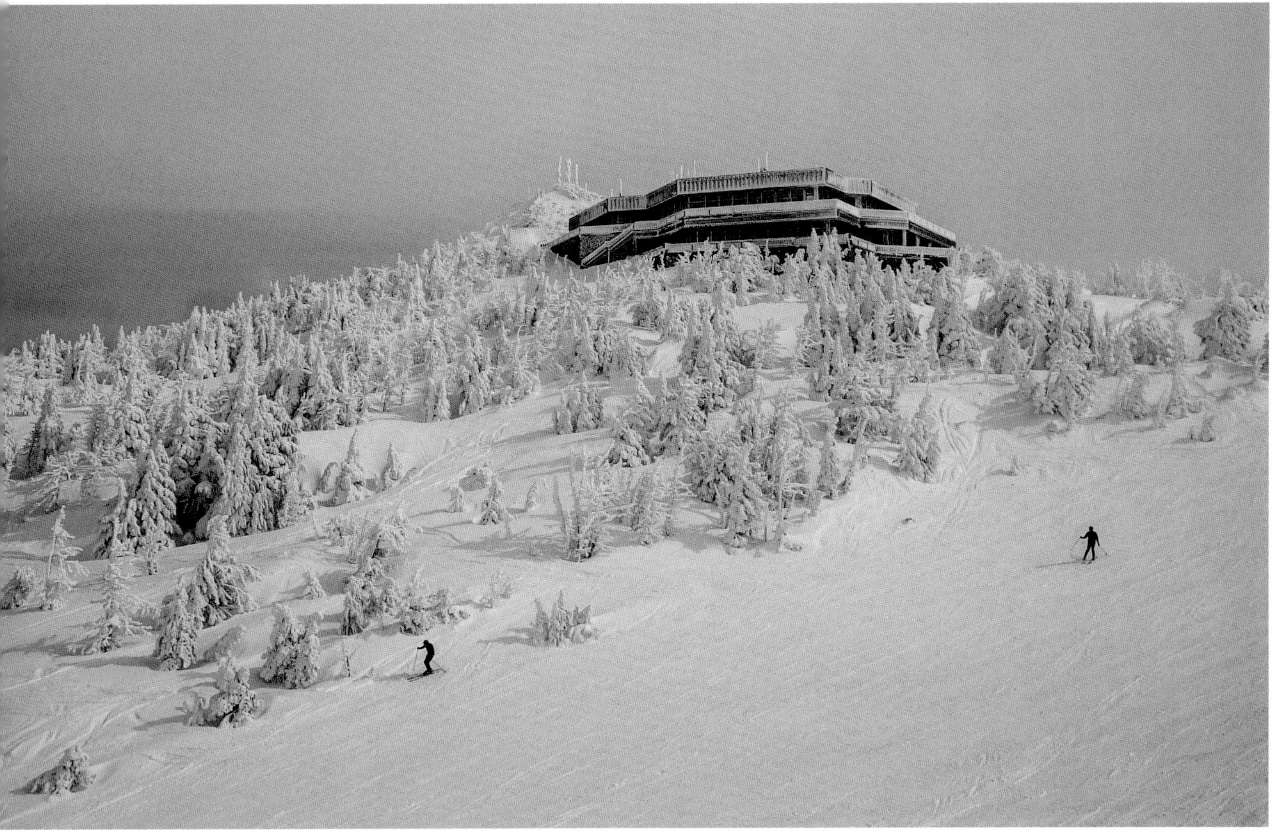

Mount Bachelor ski lodge. *Photo by George F. Peterson.*

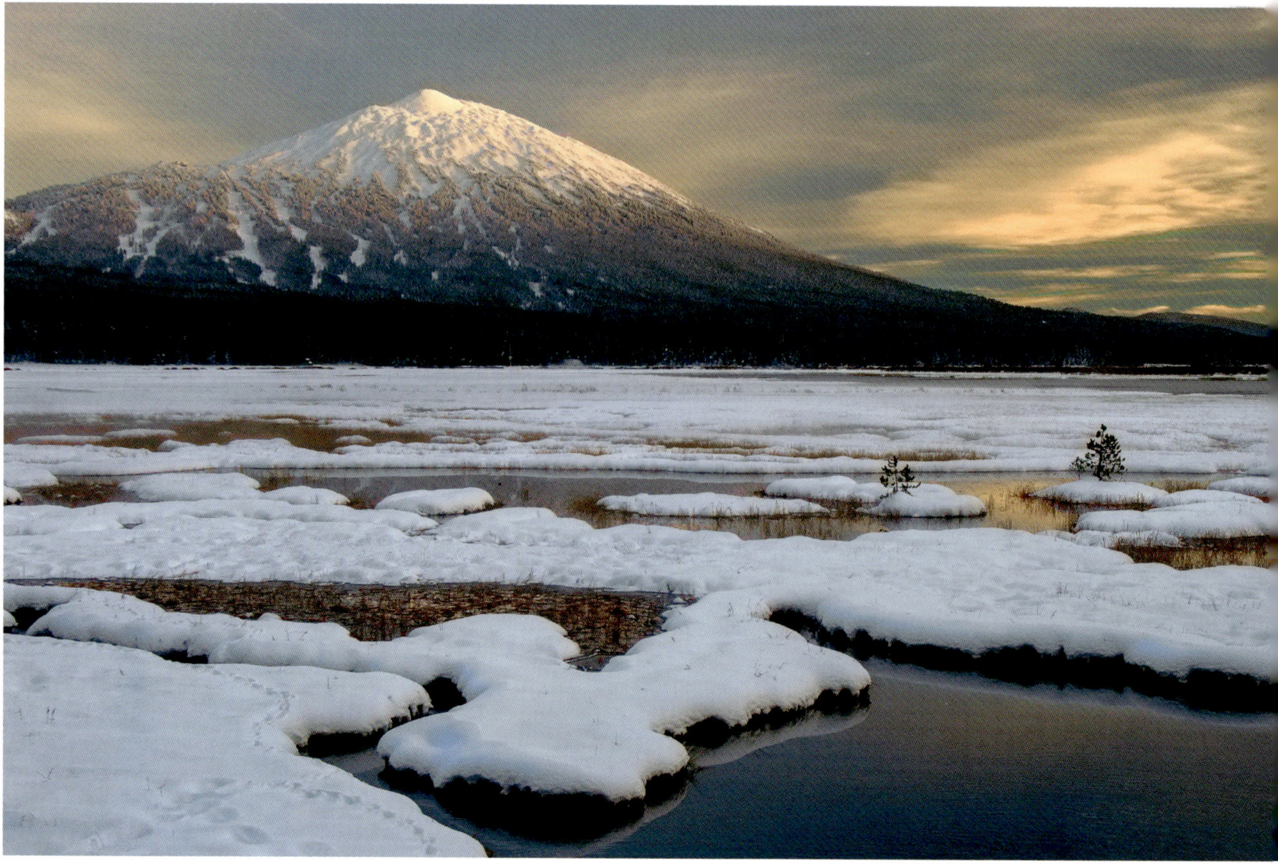

 Mount Bachelor from Sparks Lake. *Photo by Clem Paslack.*

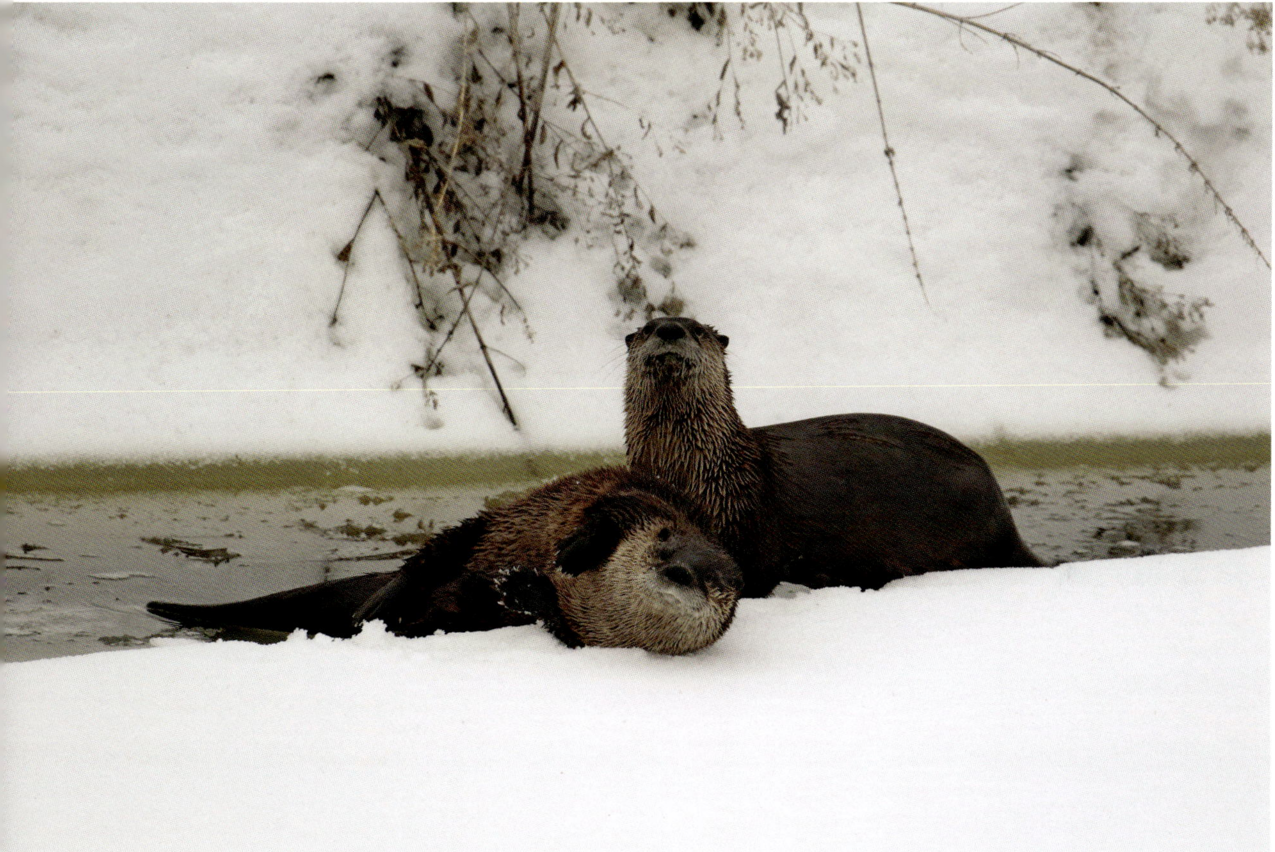

River otter in the snow. *Photo by Dan Elster.*

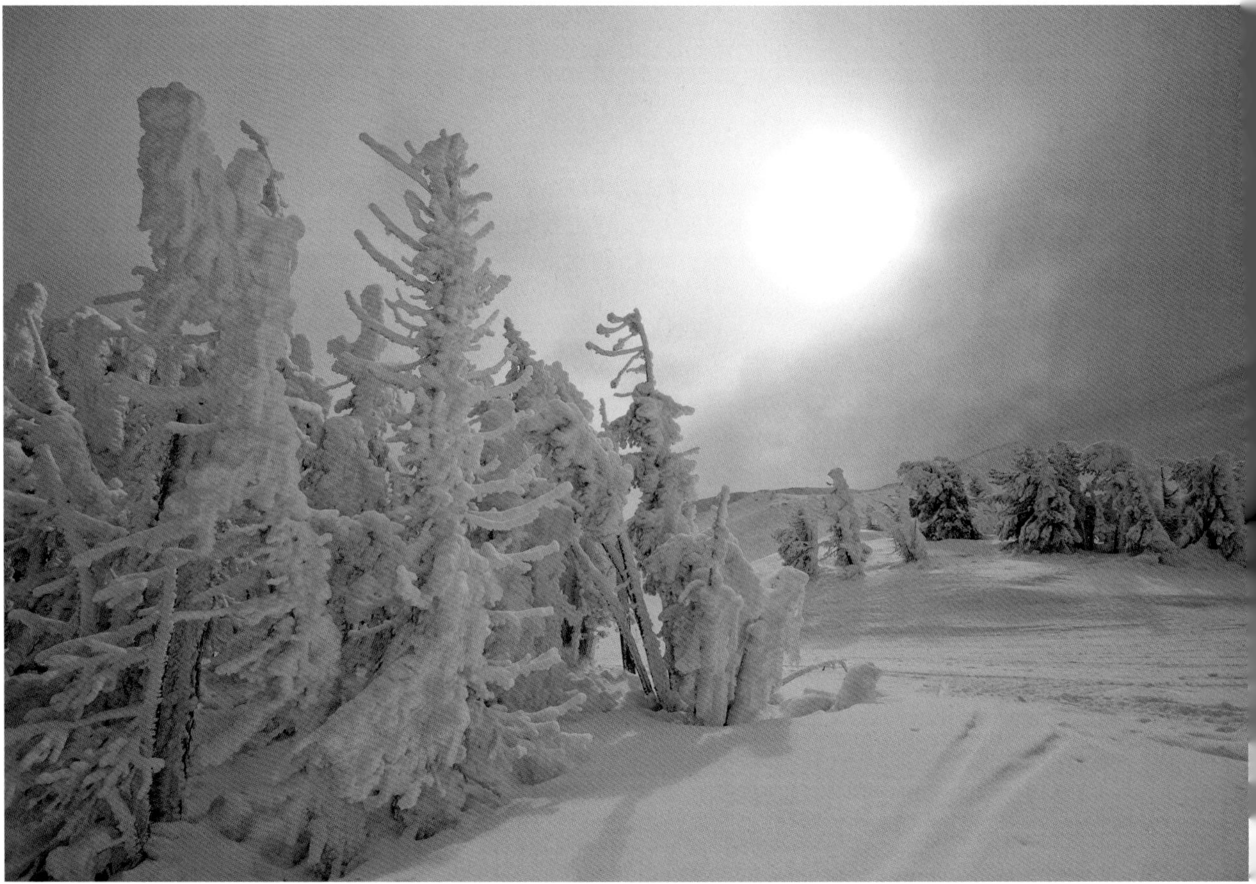

 Winter at Mount Bachelor. *Photo by Clem Paslack.*

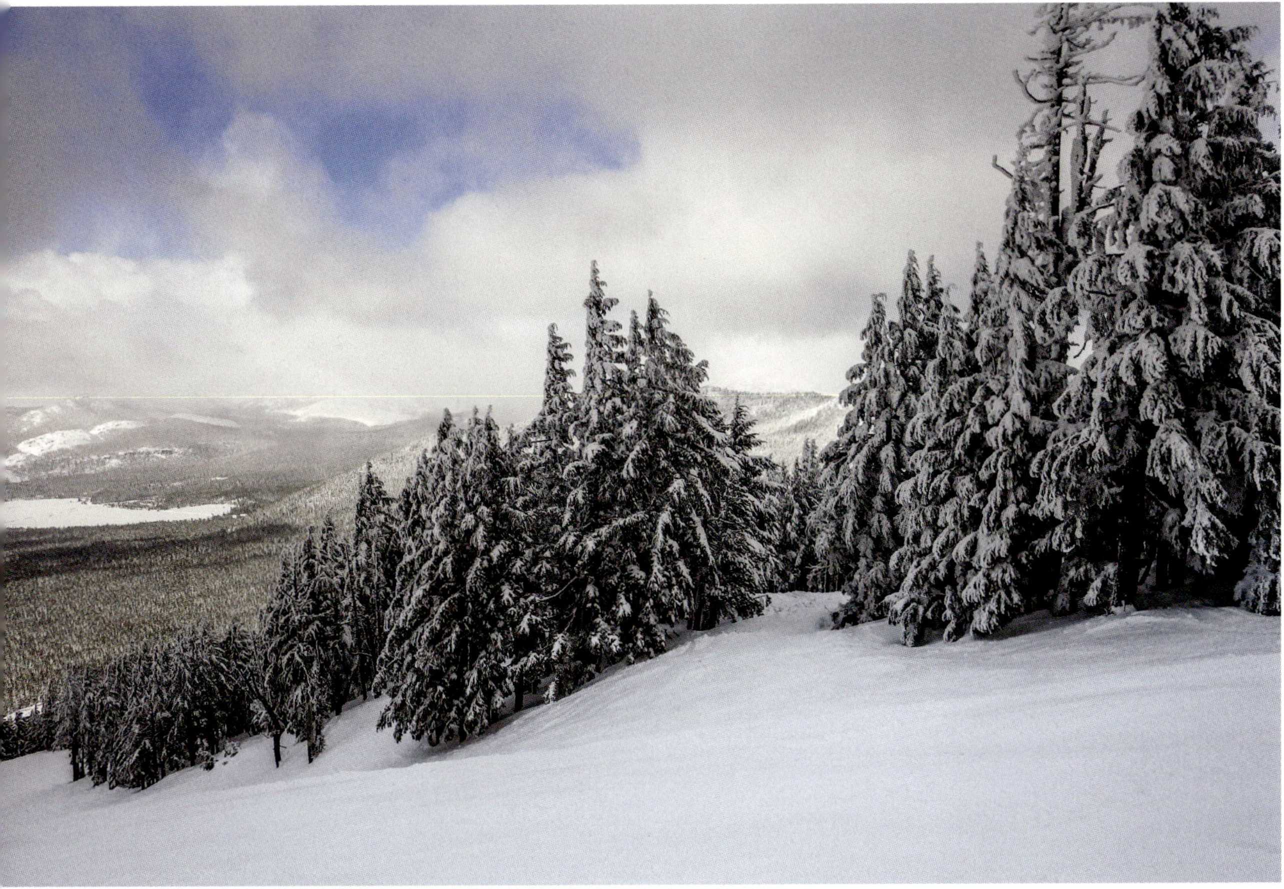

Mount Bachelor trees. *Photo by George F. Peterson.*

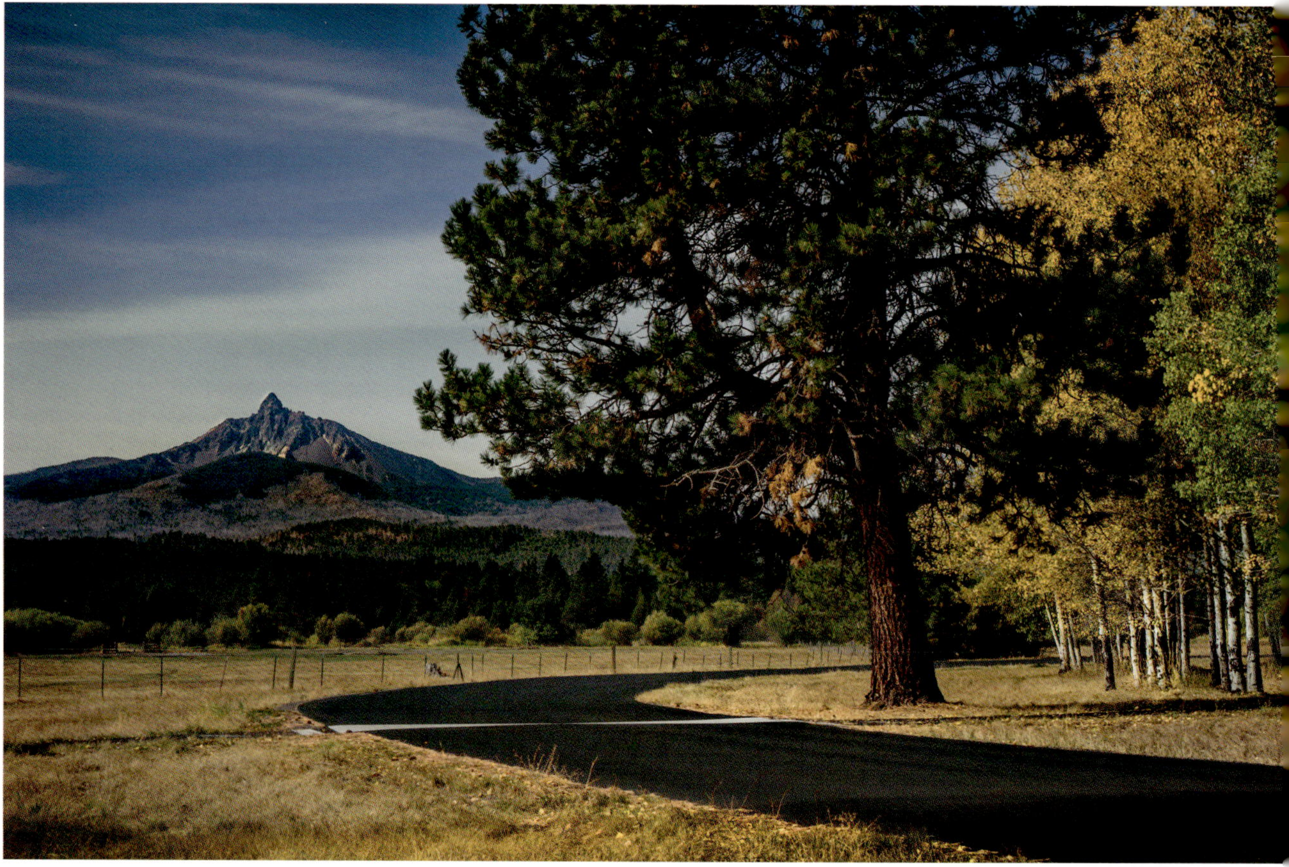

 Mount Washington from Black Butte Ranch. *Photo by Judy Benson LaNier.*

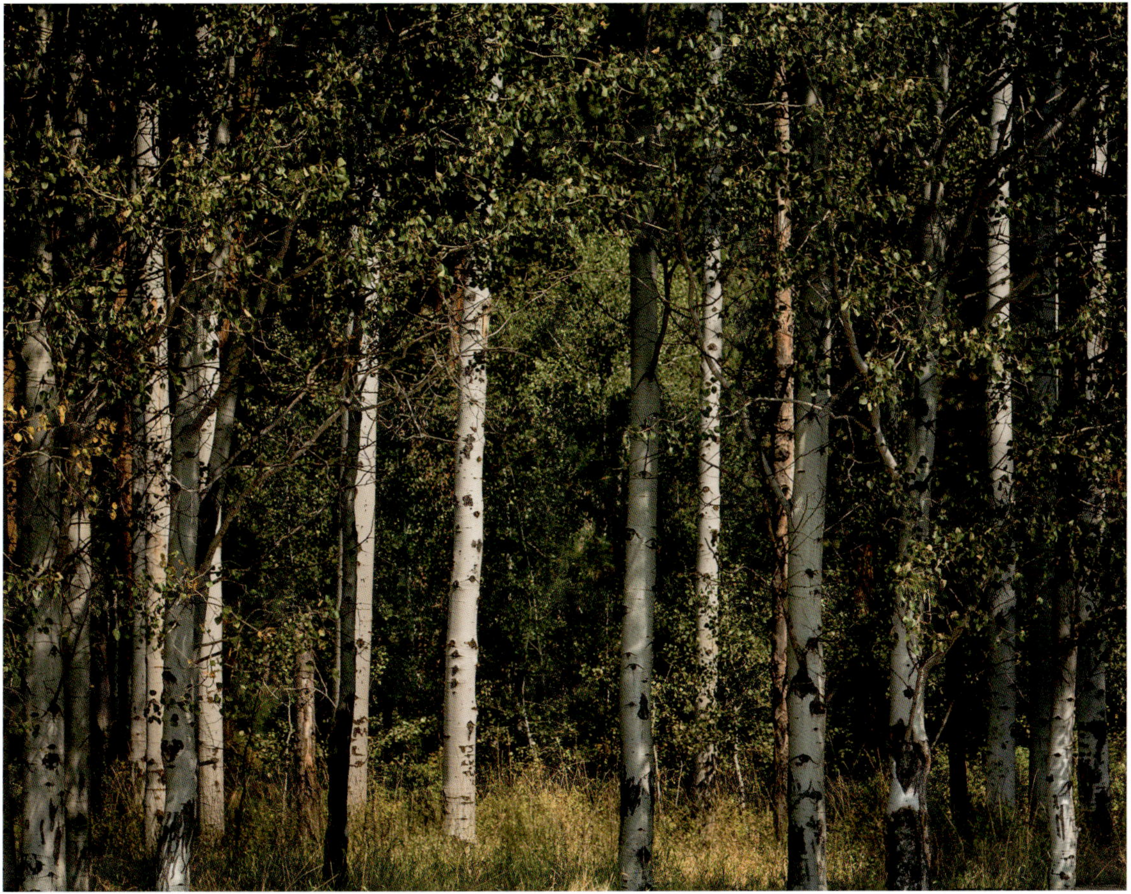

Aspens at Black Butte Ranch. *Photo by Judy Benson LaNier.*

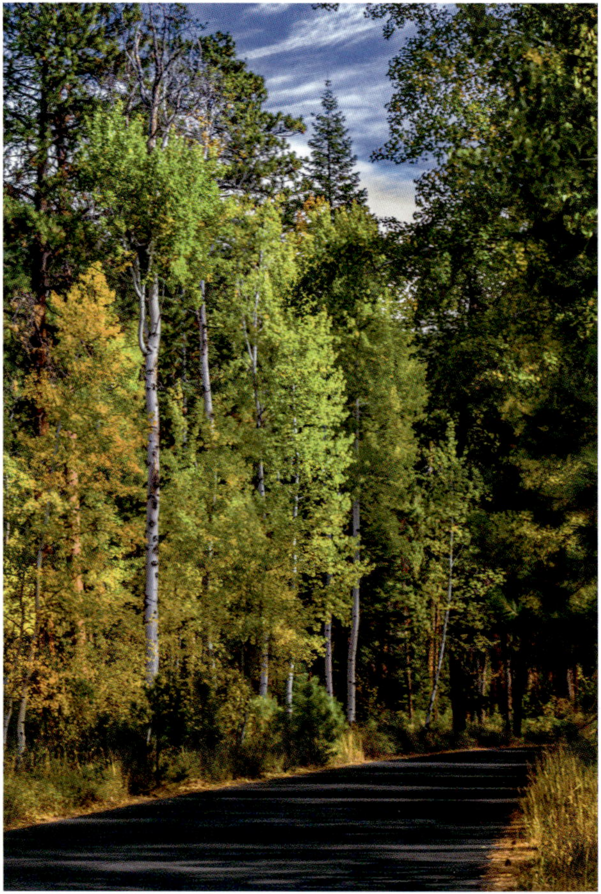

 Road to Black Butte Ranch. *Photo by Judy Benson LaNier.*

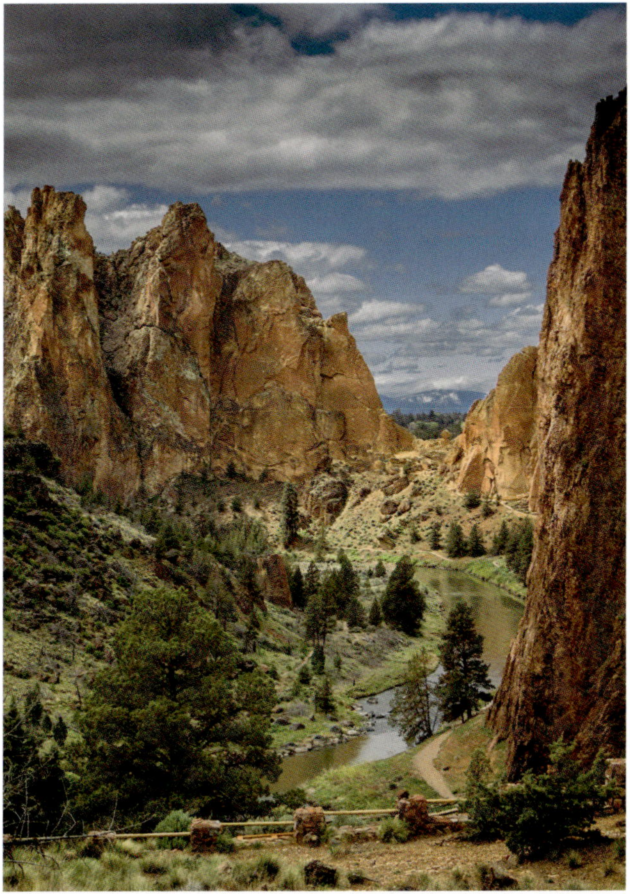

Smith Rock State Park. *Photo by Judy Benson LaNier.*

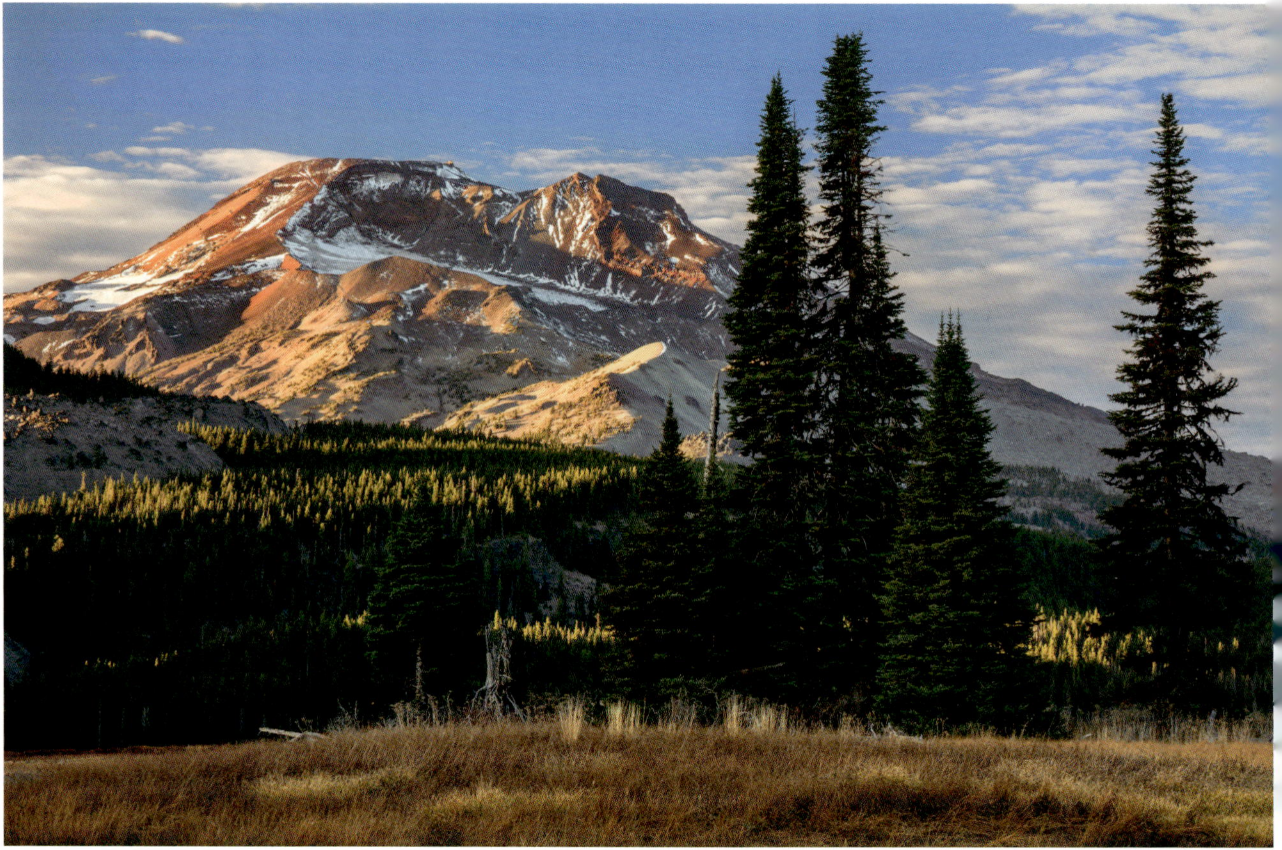

 South Sister Mountain. *Photo by Sue Newman.*

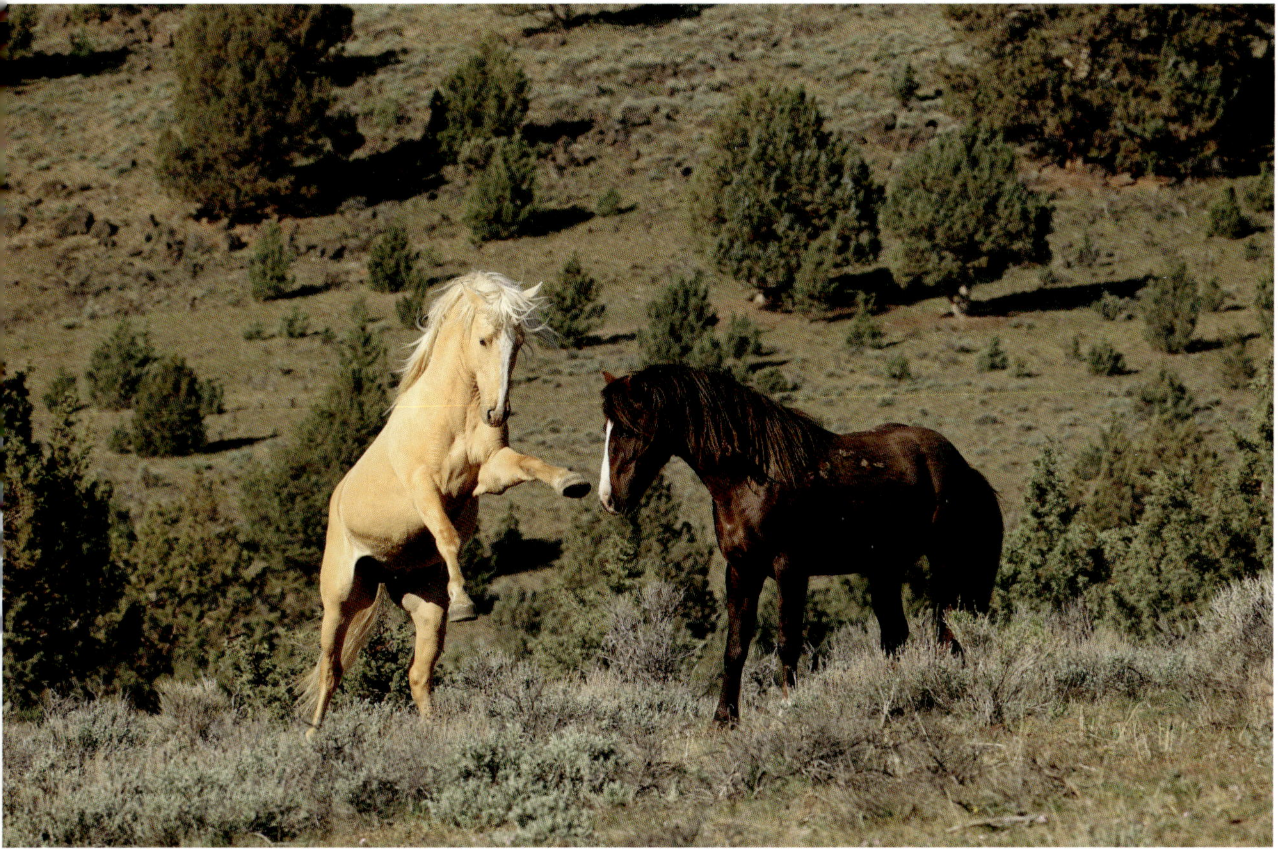

Wild horses. *Photo by Dan Elster.*

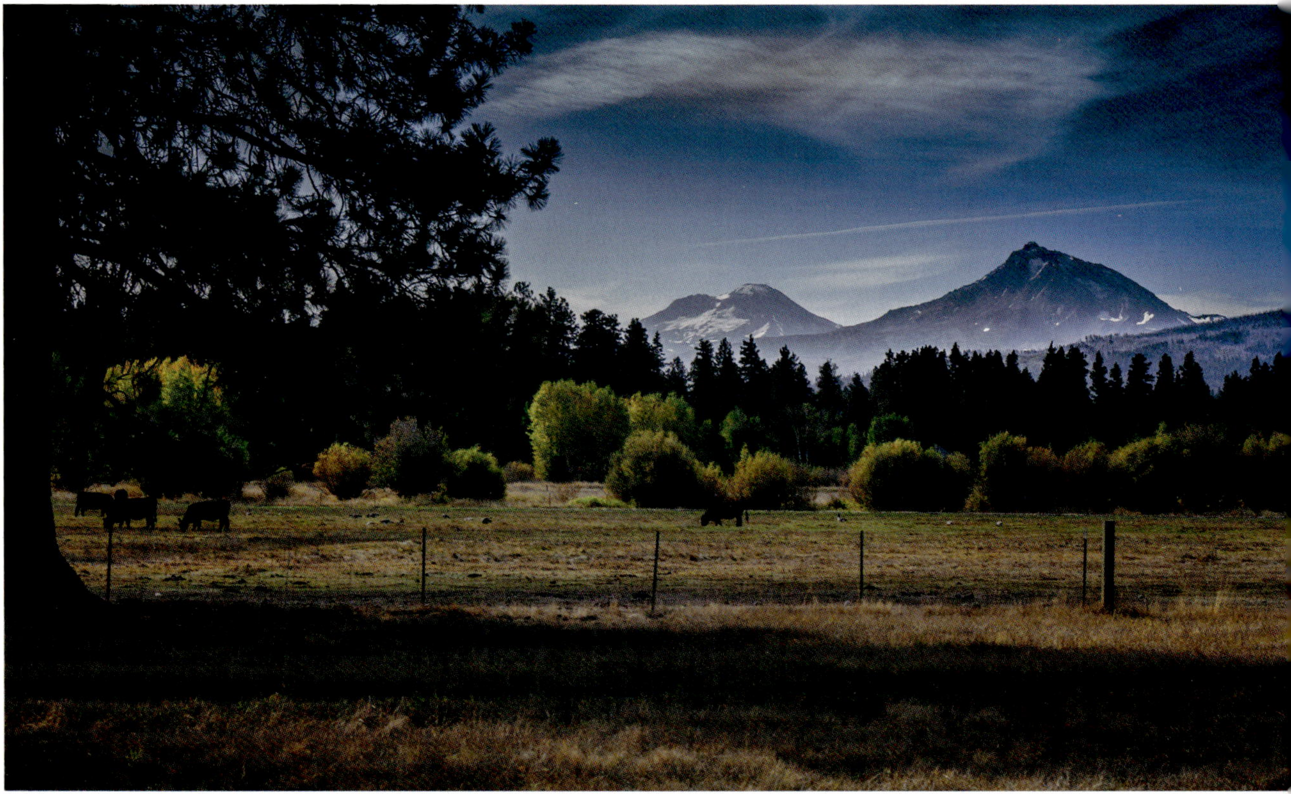

 North and South Sister Mountains from Black Butte Ranch. *Photo by Judy Benson LaNier.*

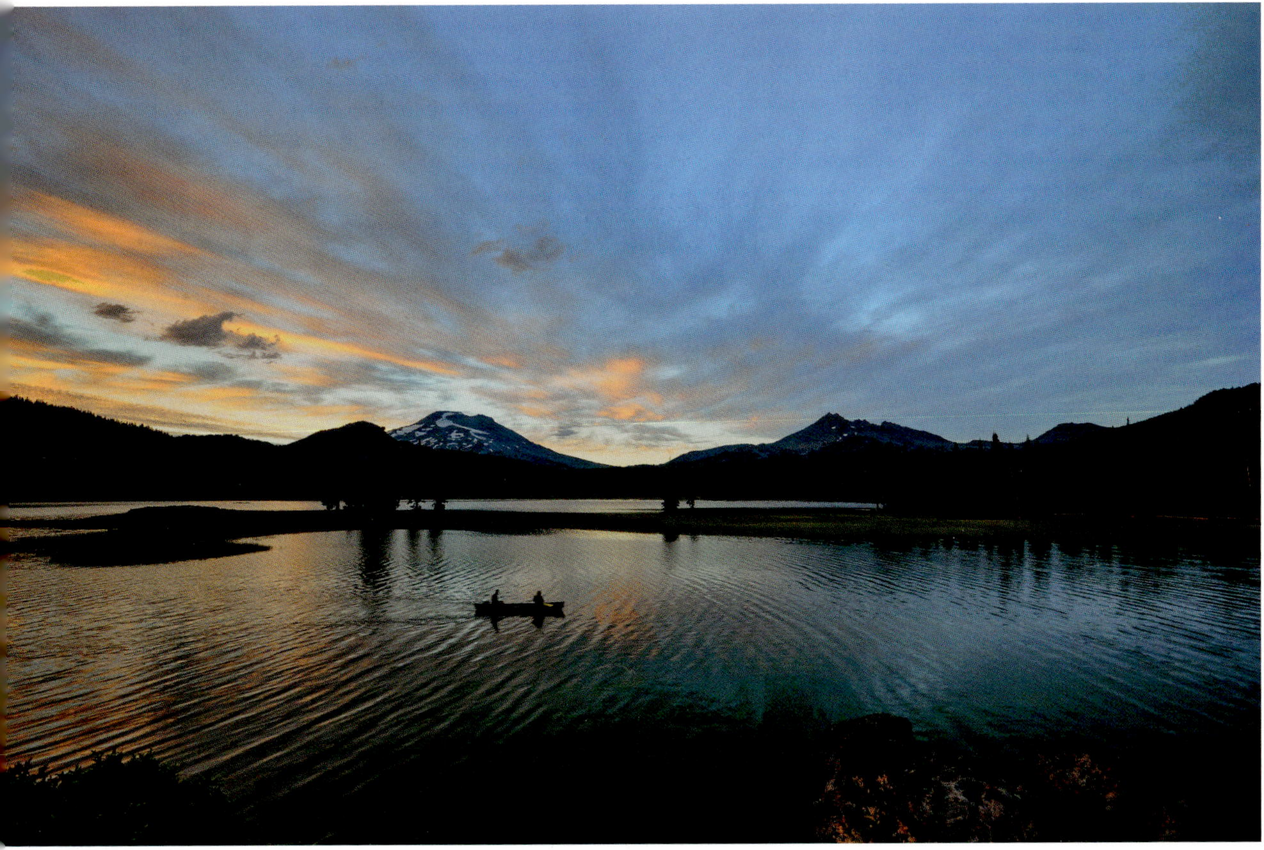

Sparks Lake. *Photo by Clem Paslack.*

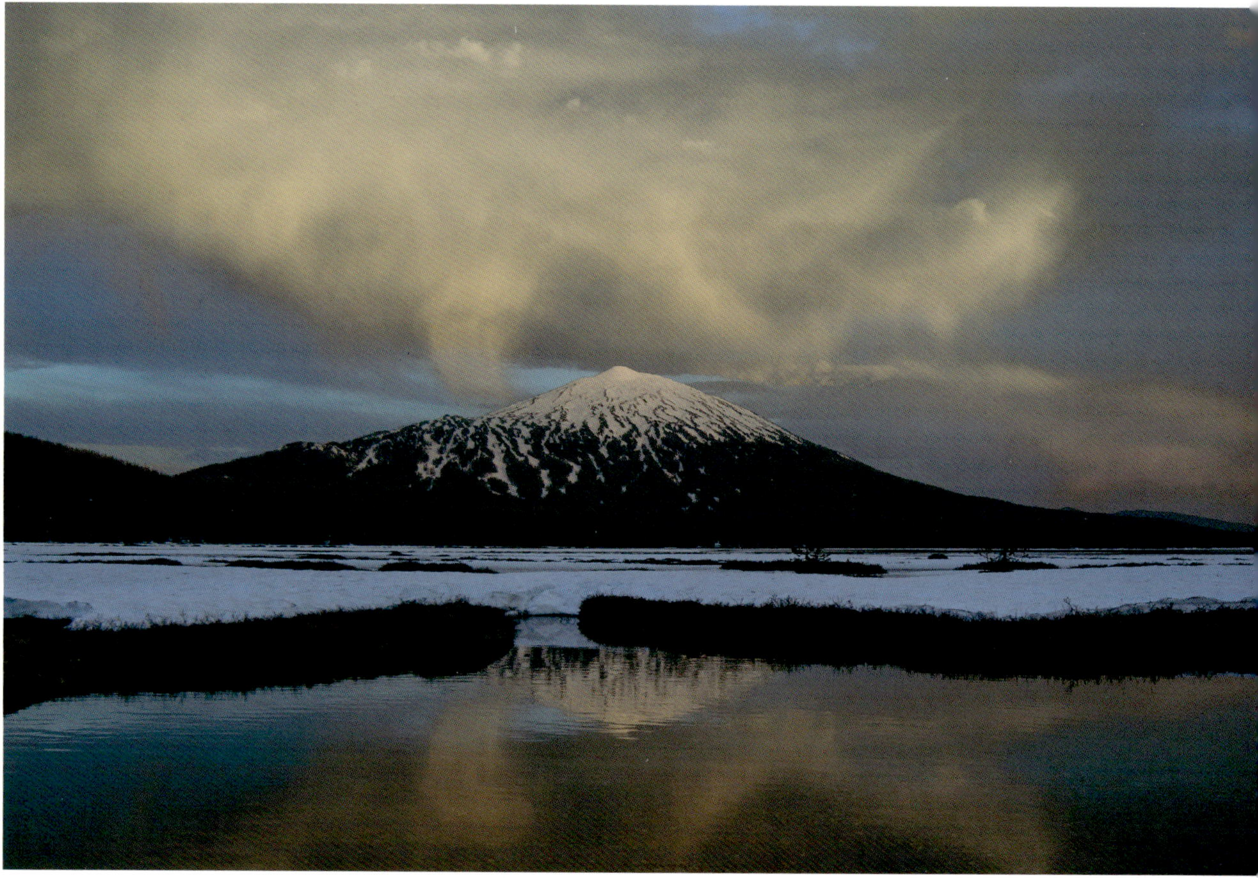

106 Clouds over Mount Bachelor. *Photo by Clem Paslack.*

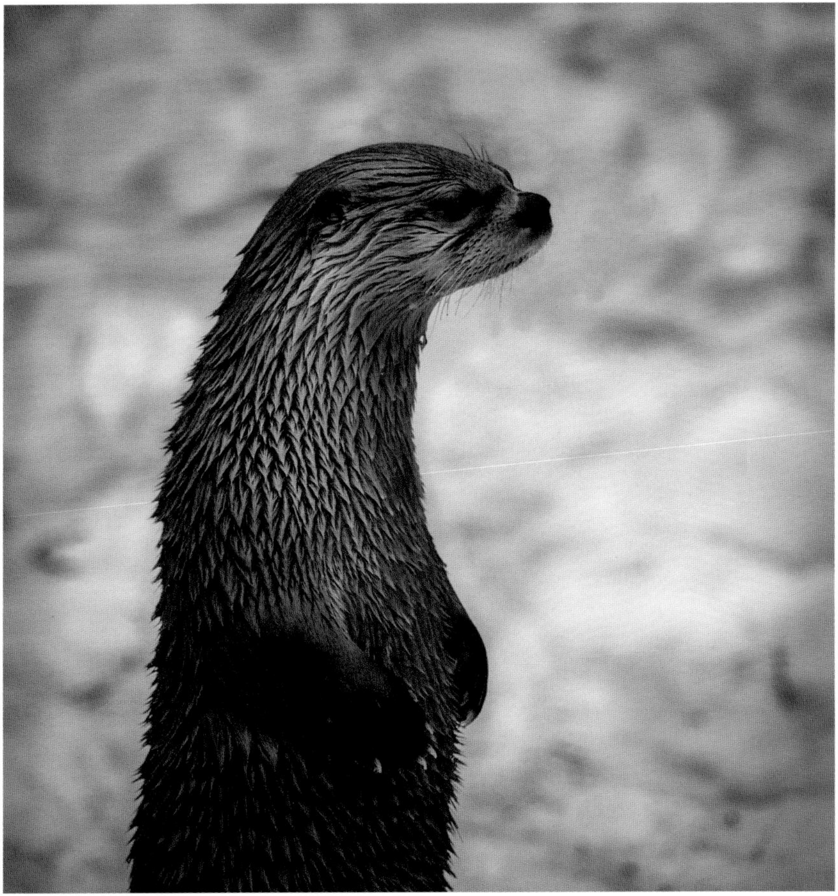

River otter, High Desert Museum. Photo by George F. Peterson.

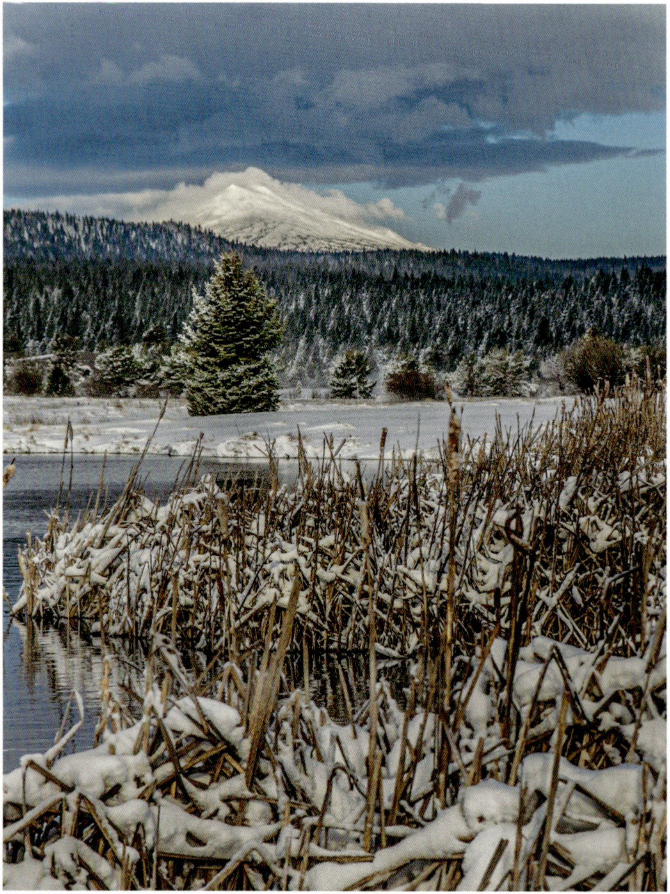

 View of Mount Bachelor from Sun River. Photo by George F. Peterson.

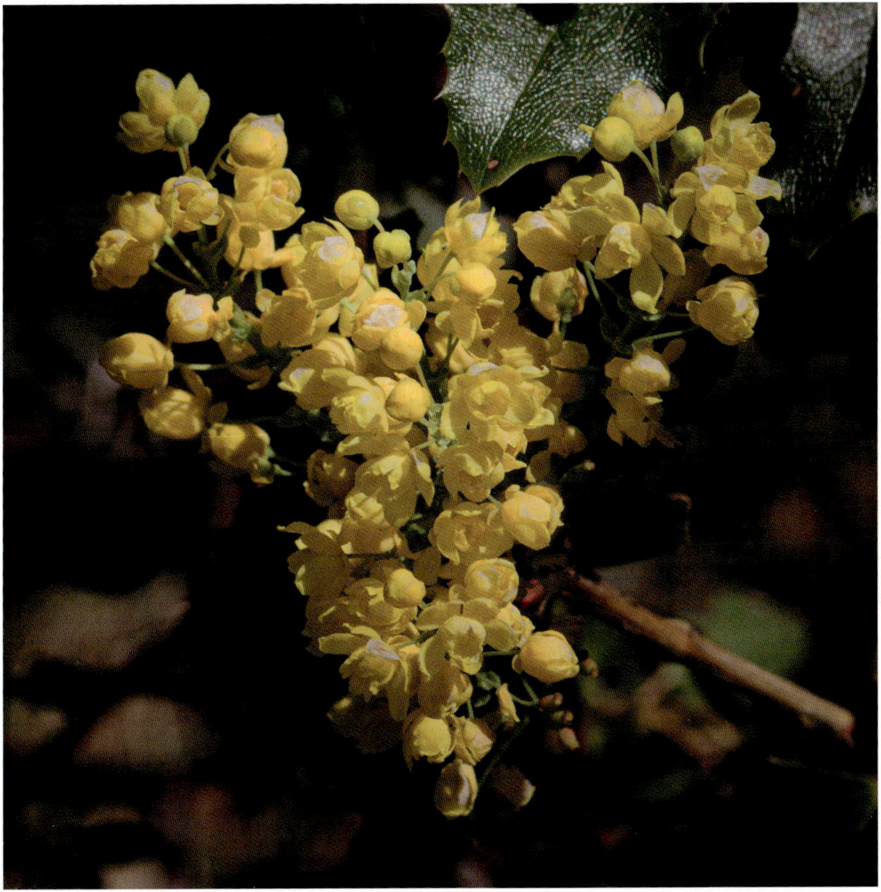

Oregon grape, the state flower of Oregon. Photo by Judy Benson LaNier.

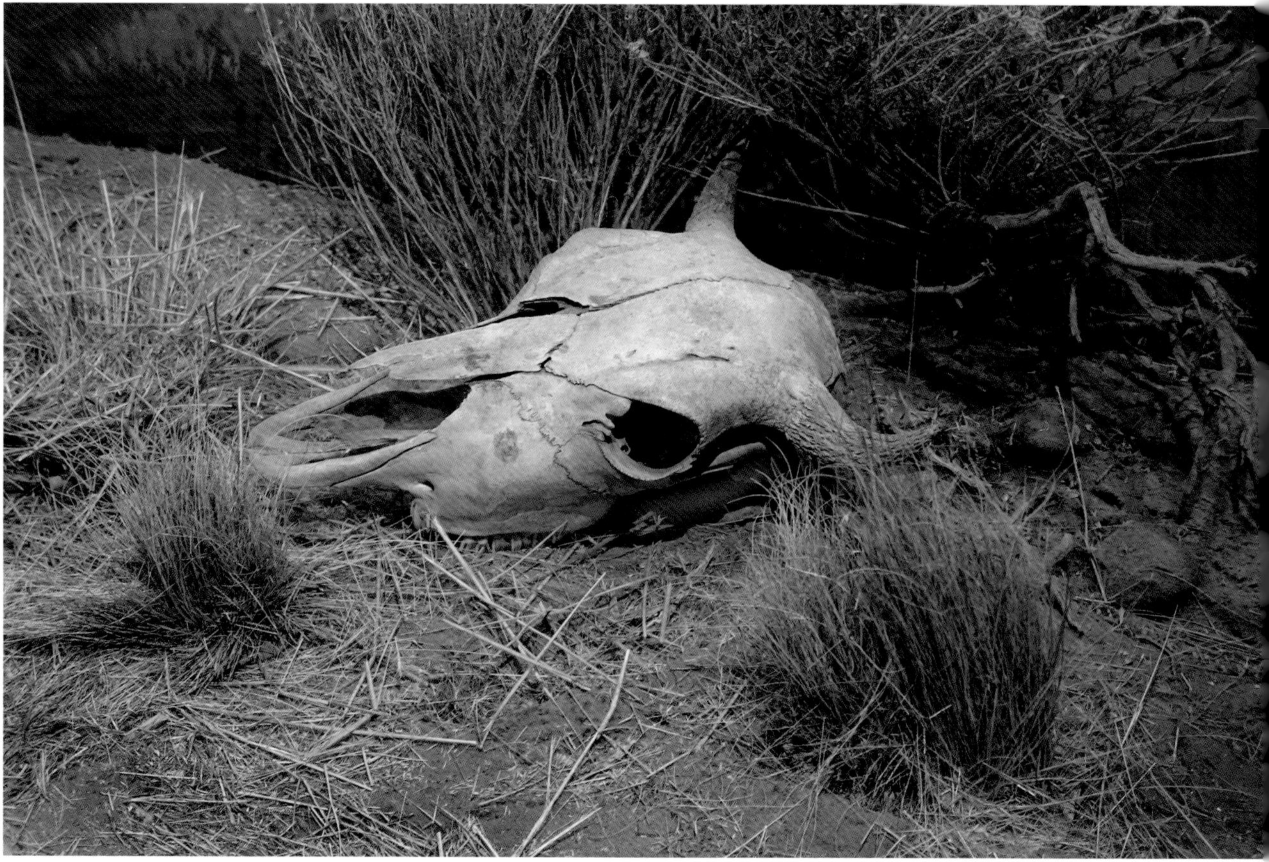

 Steer skull. Photo by Neal R. Thompson.

CREDITS

The following Oregon photographers contributed to this book.

Randy Bryan
Ken Deveney
Dan Elster
Terry Fisher
Howard Hunt
Alan Ingersoll
John Kirk
Judy Benson LaNier
Mason Marsh
Vivian McAleavey
Jay Newman
Sue Newman
Clem Paslack
George F. Peterson
John Christer Petersen
Andrea Shapiro
Diana Standing
Hans Stroo
Andrew Studer
Vldn Taylor
Neal R. Thompson
Barbara Tricarico
Nick Viani
David Lorenz Winston

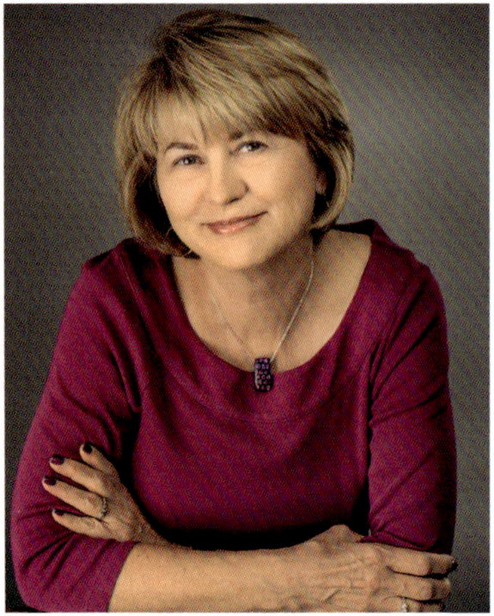

Barbara Tricarico has produced three coffee-table photography books by Schiffer Publishing: *Oregon*; *Ashland, Oregon*; and *Ashland, Oregon, Day Trips*, as well as coauthoring and photographing *Quilts of Virginia: 1607–1899*. She and her husband, Bill, moved to Ashland in 2010. Barbara is an active member of the Ashland Chamber of Commerce, is president of the Southern Oregon Photographic Association, and volunteers for the Ashland Food Project and the Oregon Shakespeare Festival. Barbara enjoys traveling and quilting. Follow her on Facebook at Barbara Tricarico Photography or visit her website, www.barbaratricarico.com.

Photo: Cornelius Matteo